Unify

We Are One

Sonia Ahmed

UNIFY BOOKS

CONTENTS

Unify In Different Languages

توحيد Arabic

Verenig Africaans

Միավորել Armenian

birləşdirmək Azerbaijani

bateratzeko Belarucian

ঐক্যসাধন করা Bengali

Унифицира Bulgarian

Unificar Catalan

统一 Chinese simplified

統一 Chinese Traditional

Ujediniti Croatian

Sjednotit Czench

Forene Danish

Verenigen Dutch

Unify English

Unuigi Esperanto

Ühendama Estonian

Bigkisin Filipino

Yhtenäistää Finnish

Unifier French

Unificar Galician

გაერთიანებულიყო Georgian

Vereinheitlichen German

Ενοποιήσει Greek

ક૨વ Gujarati

Inifye Haitian Creole

להאחיד Hebrew

एकत क करन Hindi

Egyesít Hungarian

Unify Icelandic

Menyatukan Indonesian

Irish Irish

Unificare Italian

統一する Japanese

ಒಗ್ಗೂಡಿಸು Kannada

하나로하다 Korean

Unify Lao

Uniendis Latin

Vienādot Latvian

Suvienodinti Lithuanian

Обединување Macedonian

Menyatukan Malay

Unifikati Maltenese

Forene Nowegian

کردن متحد Persian

Ujednolicić Polish

Unifica Romanian
Унифицировать Russian
Ујединити Serbian
Zjednotiť Slovak
Poenotili Slovenian
Unificar Spanish
Kuunganisha Swahili
Förena Swedish

கூட்டா Tamil

చపిక Telugu

รวมกัน Thai
Birleştirmek Turkish
Уніфікувати Ukrainian
یکجا Urdu
thống nhất Vietnamese
uno Welsh
פֿאַרייניקן Yiddish

one infinitely mathematically

INTRODUCTION

When I decided to write this book, I had always thought of a thousand reasons why I should or shouldn't do it. One of the things I thought of was the cost. I wanted a well-illustrated book with a nice cover to attract attention. I even thought about studying psychology or obtaining a certificate so that people would take the message in this book seriously, coming from a person who has a higher educational degree so people would have some kind of respect or admiration towards it because of who had written it. But again these were all types of excuses to stop me from writing it. In a way I was constantly fighting with myself because I truly did not want to write this book. However, something in my mind told me in reality it didn't matter who the book came from because even if it came from someone with an admirable profession, it would still be questioned the same way. Currently this is just the way I am, one with all the mistakes and the one with good intentions, like anyone. With that being said, I should let it be. Like a song, some people will relate to it and it will have a special meaning which will make sense to them, but it may not make sense to others.

The appearance of the book did not matter because its purpose was the most important part. This is when I knew it was time to write this book. Initially the name of this book was going to be Sequences of Life. When I started writing the Sequence of Life it was just a positive book with positive thoughts that I wanted to share with people because I was seeing a lot of negativity around me, my family, my close friends and my surroundings. A lot of my friends were discouraging me from writing this book, just as great ideas in general are diluted and eventually completely vanished without knowing what the end results would have been.

Although I had a weird feeling that made me double think whether I should do it or not, something inside me said I needed to do it. It was a necessity I needed to obey. It was something like when you tell someone you need to do something and if you don't do it, it has to be whether you want it or not. For example, when you tell your son to help you clean the kitchen and he says, "No, I can't. I have something to do." He starts giving you all kind of reasons and in the end they are only excuses to not do it.

At that moment, the voices in my mind said don't do it if you don't want to, but it will still be, no matter what. I wanted to say no. I felt a force within me, it was something telling me "Even if I don't want to do it, I'll have to do it anyway because it is necessary for it to happen."

At that moment I understood that it was not me who had to do it, it was not me who had control over this. By thinking of it that way it was impossible for me to make it happen, to tell the world about my dream, about unifying ourselves. It was necessary because it was something we all knew in our subconscious. At the end of it all that was the reason behind our daily fight with our selves. At the end of it all, I felt that by bringing peace to everyone, without hate, was the only way I could reach everyone without discrimination.

This is when I realized that my parents had wanted me to be independent of the opinions of others in order to achieve what I had always wanted to do in my life. And because of that reason that I needed to be myself however, I understand that I needed to be independent from the minds of others, but never independent of God because God was and is constantly communicating to me in my thoughts and in my feelings. I asked myself why this was necessary. I instantly got an answer that it was because every individual person is a world with their own dreams.

Everyone has their own reasons of being special just as I did, but not for the same reason in which I was called. To identify what is logical in this world for one person may not necessarily be logical to the other. Everyone has that special call which shouts from within, that frustrated call which we ignore with logic by constantly giving ourselves excuses for not listening to our inner self. I suggest you not get frustrated. Find yourself by meditating and not looking in the outside in the opinions of others, because if this was the case, this book would not have been written entirely. Learn to think by quieting your mind and listening to your thoughts because they will always have something to tell you.

For instance, I was driving towards my office and decided to turn the radio but somehow the radio station was tuned to a foreign Vietnamese station which is a language I do not understand. My reaction was to change the radio station but before I could do so, my cell phone rang. This distracted me from getting to change that radio station. The strange part was, there was no one on the other end of the call. So I put the phone down and continued where I left off- back to wanting to change that radio station but then there was a thought that came to me which was not coming from my own thinking. This "thought" said "wait, don't change the radio station" but then my answer was me thinking of why should I listen to what I do not understand. It was not logical to listen to something that makes no sense to me. Knowing there is a difference between a "thought" and "thinking", I allowed myself to listen to that thought. I identified that thought to be words from God. As I listen to the words from that thought that said to me "I know this does not make sense to you right now, to listen to this radio station, but I need for you to do it until you reach your office". My office was approximately another 10 minutes of driving so I continued to listen to it even though it made absolutely no sense to me.

Once I reached my office, I stopped and parked and that thought came to me ,again, saying, "What did you understand?" I answered within myself that I did not understand anything with the exception of the word "cell phone" which seemed like cell phone advertising. That thought then said to me "that is the point." I answered by saying I still don't understand. That thought answered back by saying "this is how some people will understand your message at first". This made me aware that I don't need to get frustrated when I come across those who do not get it; it is nothing for me to take personally. It's understandable that an average person would not be able to digest this at first because it is just not easy to understand until you are able to think beyond your own thoughts.

For instance, when I started writing the book, I honestly thought I was doing it myself. Then, I realized I was only asking the questions and our Creator was giving me the answers of what to write in the book. During the beginning of this year in the month of February, there was about a week that he taught me to see beyond what I was able to see. Just as if you are driving a car and focusing only on the car in front of you, this blocks you from seeing beyond that car and being aware of your surroundings. He also taught me how to hear beyond what I was able to hear before. For instance, when you are having a conversation with another person you concentrate on the subject of that conversation but hearing beyond that conversation is listening to the tone and what is not being said. He taught me how to think beyond how I was able to think before. Just as I mentioned earlier on how to distinguish the difference between a "thought" and just your normal "thinking" – the "thought "are answers from God and "thinking" is figuring out the answer yourself. He also taught me to feel beyond what I was able to feel before. Depending on the feeling either it be good or bad, it's connected with the "thoughts". So if the thought created a bad feeling, it is not coming from God. Or from GOOD, or it will not have a positive energy.

It is understandable that this could all be overwhelming but don't get frustrated, find yourself and you will know that life is beautiful. The purpose of this book started in my mind because I wanted to find the truth to everything with knowing that only God could answer the truth I was seeking. Before asking God for the truth, I asked the people around me what they thought about God and who he really is. They replied with different answers, and in a way I knew they were all correct because they had their own version of what God means to them. So, I asked God, "What is your truth?" I was open to his answers. I asked outside of my own opinion because after listening to everyone's truth, I had formed my own truth. It was based on real life, the life I was addicted to live based on everyone else's truth and I felt like we were all just going around in circles, staying in the same place. We were all without exception on the same boat. That is the truth I want you to know.

Subconsciously, through meditation, and in my dreams I have learned the truth we are all looking for, the truth we can only find within ourselves. When we do find it, there will be no need for an explanation because the truth will fall under its own weight like the law of gravity within us. When you learn that truth, you will look beyond races, nationalities, or social classes in people. When that happens within us, there will no longer be grudges, there will no longer be fear, there will no longer be jealousy, nothing will harm you and you'll feel like you are on a cloud right here on earth. This is the awakening. Your body doesn't matter anymore on earth. You'll start living the eternal life in this life because you have the internal peace. When you feel this peace, you'll start living in harmony. You'll understand everything because you'll learn to see people like yourself in your reflection and you will not want to hurt anyone.

In the near future, put yourself in place of the poor person who doesn't even have shoes because they don't have money to spend. Next, put yourself in a place of someone who doesn't have legs and therefore doesn't even have feet to put shoes on. Look in the mirror and put yourself in the place of someone who doesn't have food. When I say to put yourself in that place of that person, actually live their life for one day. Naturally, with no food, that person will not be able to feed themselves. Fast that day and dedicate this to those who do not have food to eat. Dedicate that day to them however; don't forget that person probably doesn't have water either. So, for that day, don't drink water. Don't worry about not eating or drinking for one day, your organs will be okay. You won't die of one day of hunger or one day of thirst, but there are people who do die of continuous hunger and thirst. This will help you become conscious of others and will help you appreciate everything, beginning with food and water. For one day, go to the hospital and observe the children, who have cancer or other terminal illnesses, it will help you to be thankful for your health. For one day, go see the elderly. Spend the day with them because if our creator permits it, you'll know this will be the last step before your life ends here on earth. You'll learn how important it is to live every moment, from moment to moment. You'll learn to appreciate not only every day, but every moment as well. If you put yourself on the other side of the mirror, you will no longer be capable of offending anyone because you'll know that you're on the other side of the mirror as well and God is in every body without discrimination and anything you say or do will be reflected back to you. When we all learn this, even slaves will cease to be their own slaves because they will be freed from all chains.

1 WHEN I WAS A LITTLE GIRL

When I was a child I use to meditate. This may sound strange or unusual but every child does actually meditate because God has been in us from day one. Everything was so natural, like when a kid dances or runs or laughs because it was something that was already natural to me. Now that I think back to that time, I did not know that I was meditating and what actual meditating really was. As a child I used to live in a small town and enjoyed watching water fall upon the trees and flowing down upon the leaves when looking out from my window. I always had that question, how certain things happen, was always on my mind. I had a book that was given to me by my mother which was a book of stamp collections. This book was full of questions and the stamps were to be found in snacks to solve the questions. So in order to

11

find the answers, I had to buy a certain snack to find the answers to the questions that were in the book. This book was titled <u>The Reason Why Things Happen Scientifically Speaking</u>. This gave me more knowledge and a better understanding of why things happen when those questions in the book were answered.

When I was a little girl, my mother one day explained to me in her own way that there was a God and that even though I couldn't see him, he could see me. She also told me that even though I couldn't hear him talk like she or someone else did to me, I could hear him in my mind. I remember when she said this to me I asked her, "Why can't I see him, Mommy?" Her answer was that he is so grand and big that our eyes are too little to see him. She went on explaining that he was very good to everyone because he loved us so much that whenever we asked him for anything he would give it to us, but only when he thought it was the right time. Keeping that in mind, I went to the garden in my house where there were many fruit trees; it was a spacious place to play in. Even though I had toys, sometimes I didn't want to play with them. There were times when I would rather play with the sticks on the ground or the different types of stones around me or even just play with dirt. I remember sitting down and observing an ant's nest and at that moment I remembered what my mother had said to me. I thought about how God was so big that we couldn't see him. The questions of how and why all went through my mind. Many times I imagined that to God we were like ants because he could see where we came from and where we were going to. The ants can't see me, but I can see them. I am enormously big to them; they struggle to survive just like us. Try to experiment what I had just explained to you and look at an army of ants by putting your finger near one of them and they will continue to walk unbothered, without even noticing they are straying from their path. Then, ask yourself, do they really see you and know who you are or do they think you are part of the new path? Do they really know you led it astray? Ask yourself that moment and observe. You can see the ant, but it can't see you. Try to understand how God can oversee us all, with the exception that in the case of our creator everything is deeper because he can see into our eyes, listen through our ears, and know our thoughts. I remember many times I played with the ants as a little girl. I remember there were ants carrying a crumb of food trying to climb uphill. I picked it up with a small twig to try and help it reach its destination more easily but I then realized the ant had gone back to its original place. It didn't look too happy; it was as if it wanted to do things on its own, not appreciating my help. The ant also did not notice the twig I used to help it up and where it had come from. I later told myself how regularly rain came down in that place and that puddles often formed there, as they do during floods. I asked myself what it must be like for ants when it rains or when there was wind. I thought it must be much like a hurricane or a flood. Do they know where it comes from and how things happen? As I thought of that I realized an ant's world is one of survival, just like us. We only think of ourselves every day, of what we're going to do and what we're going to eat. However, we know there is someone more powerful than us who has authority over us. We hold a certain respect knowing that there are limits to our abilities as humans and the limits we have as individuals. We know there is someone beyond our understanding. We know that for him, our creator, there are no limits.

I played with the ants and when I blew hard I noticed some were blown away with the force of my breath. I then asked myself, "What happened?" Again, they did not notice it had been me who had blown air towards them even though I imagine some of them had been hurt by my breath. I then began to think the air I had blown, to them, had been like a hurricane. It was something out of their control and I continued to play with them. Later, I thought about what would happen if I dropped water on them with something like a sieve to see if they knew where it was coming from. Some got wet, others ran off to another place, but they didn't know what it was about. They didn't know it was me who had drizzled water over them. I could see them, but they couldn't see me because they were too busy with their daily routine. All they knew was that water was falling and it was windy. Then, it occurred to me to get some crumbs of bread for them to carry home. Some of them immediately grabbed their crumbs of bread, but still did not realize who had in that moment given them those pieces of bread. Neither did they try to figure out who was there, I noticed while I observed them the whole time. The only thing that mattered to them at that moment was that they were living without worrying about how it was getting to them. To me that was a very fun day, but I could imagine how God was acting with us and I knew that even though I couldn't see him, he could see me. Even if I tried, my sight was not able to capture so far as to allow me to see him. He, however, could see where I was coming from, where I was going to, and what my way of thinking was. We all know an ant only thinks about survival and the current moment in which it is living because of that I believe there is a lot of similarity between the ants and us. Irrelevant to what we believe, we are all vulnerable to many things without realizing it and we are all in his hands.

2 LOGICAL WORLD

The message of this book is to make you aware that we are one, just a reflection of each other, coming from one, and being one. And when we separate each other we feel left out or like we are leaving someone out. We start wondering if we are right and they are wrong or if we are wrong and they are right. This feeling comes because we separate ourselves when we are not supposed to. What we don't realize is that everyone hurts the same when we see a child suffer or an elder. It hurts everyone equally when there is injustice or malice when we think at a humane level. When we separate from God, we think we don't need him and start having feelings of competition, like we need to be better than the rest. We think we can do everything without God, but thinking that way is allowing our EGO to take over our life, because being without GOD in a way is, being hopeless.

Deep inside yourself, you know there is someone who started all this. If you question yourself, with all these ideas in your mind it may be illogical like there is no end. You will have more and more questions. If you notice all the prophets brought a message with them and the message was that there is one God. All of it was put into some type of a test where all of them were questioned. Some of them had to demonstrate with something that God was true. If we stop and think about it, God is already doing this in different ways with us. That is why everything we find impossible is not. The impossible is something that has not yet been discovered by man. "Discovery" means it was there and it was just hidden until someone uncovered it. If you look around you and observe everything discovered by man, it is a miracle of life. Nobody could believe it existed until someone with firm faith came along and discovered. Even though there were contradictions, he persevered and finally made it visible to everyone.

(Even after they proved it according to their capacity)
Just for the record to let people know when I was writing the book I always ask God our creator for help to correct the mistakes and in this book. In this case,

this line that now is in parenthesis was a line that God helped me correct because I was wrong in the explanation that I was giving. You may ask yourself how God helped me correct that line in the book. For more explanation on this, see the chapter of Miracles.

What I meant to say was that everyone, all the prophets including Jesus, wanted to demonstrate God exists with their own capacity. That was wrong because no one is capable of doing anything without the spirit of God. It was never their own capacity. In a way, we are like a glove and God is the hand. The glove cannot move or do anything without the hand like in the case of John of God. John of God from Brazil is a healer, in our eyes, but he is actually the glove and God is the hand. We cannot see the hand, but we are seeing the glove perform those miracles. (You can watch his videos on YouTube.) We tend to judge who is performing the miracles and when we judge we negate.

In the case of Jesus, we think he was the healer, but he was also the glove. Everything was done through the Spirit of God. When we think it was Jesus, we negate God and we unable ourselves.

The Kingdom of God is the door to the knowledge of his Kingdom of how to live in harmony like Heaven on earth. For that we need to connect to our source, which is The Creator and The Provider of all. For our Creator to be our GPS, just like the Spirit was to Jesus. But even after that, it was not enough for most of them to believe that God was real because we are logical. It has to make sense for us and we want proof of everything. We always give credit to whoever is demonstrating that God exists because in reality we are not able to see God. We are only seeing the glove. We think it's the glove, but it is the hand. Sometimes what we see or live is not what we want, but we have to ignore it. We have to be illogical to what we see. If we allow ourselves to live the moment we do not like, we get into it and then suffer because we allowed our feelings to be there. I know there are some stories with which you don't identify with, you simply don't like, or you don't agree with because of what they did in their moment. However, think about it, as much as you tried to change those books of past stories, even if you rewrote them, they would not be those stories; rather they'd be the story of what you think of them.

If you ask a lawyer what he works in, his response will be: I practice law. Why does he practice laws if they are constantly changing? When a lawyer graduates, he needs to continue renewing his license after a certain time because laws from one state to the other and one country to another are not the same. Why? It is because they're based on the beliefs in that moment and place. It is because the majority believes this at that time, even if not everyone agrees. It is one by one vote to the majority. It is so until new laws are rediscovered or rewritten according to the necessities in that period of time.

Now think about when you ask a doctor about his job. His response will be: I practice medicine. Why does he practice medicine? It is because that is the truth. He practices and is practicing with you. To be truthful, they constantly continue discovering. Every day there are new things that they didn't even know about in science. That is why they are also constantly renewing their license. It is to update their knowledge. Out of curiosity, ask them about the people who have been cured of any terminal diseases. According to their point of view, they were cured by faith, or by medicine, because if you analyze it, the government changed a law in regards to the side effects of medicine. If you realize it, you'll see they are trying to change the feelings and the secondary effects, they are many more than the ones they were trying to cure. Ask yourself what has cured you, your faith or the medicine you obtained? Is it the fact that the ones who had much faith and took the medicine were cured? Why do others with the same illness not have the same result if they have taken the same medicine? Or why does the Placebo Effect work on people?

I want to ask you, if you know someone close who you know, do that favor and ask them that question, but at the same time help them understand it is God who permitted it. Even the leaf of a tree falls at the precise moment with God's will, the Creator. With us, it has to be visible in order for us to believe it. That is why we need to let things happen of their own will if it needs to be, in the form it is. Just like that, successively, distances between one place and another will be shorter, because there are now planes. It is no longer like when the prophets he sent were on earth. Communication between one side of the world and the other is not so long. You can see and talk to someone in that place effortlessly. It is all because of strength of energy because there is not a cable from one place directly to another. Before, it was through a messenger bird that was used to carry messages.

3 WHAT IS UNIFY?

I personally did not know the true meaning of Unify. My question of how Unify came to my mind was answered as I was trying to find the truth of Our Creator. It was when I made thousands of questions that seemed to me impossible to understand. I knew our Creator loved us deeply, but if that was true, why was he being so unfair by giving the truth of his words to a certain amount of people and leaving the rest of the world lost in a lie, or at least what they or others believed to be true.

It was there that I asked if everything about Jesus and other prophets was true or if somehow someone had contacted after Jesus or communicated after Jesus. My mind could not understand anything at all. Within me I knew I was missing something and I could not figure out what it was. That day in a dream while sleeping, a scene was repeated but this time in my dream he told me the truth about how we are all one. And I asked him how we could be only one if when I looked everywhere, I saw that we are so many. It was then that he explained to me in my dreams that we are all parts, but when we see the other we are just a reflection. We came to be from one and were formed not by mistake, but on purpose and we are living an illusion of everything. We see everything but the truth. That is what we do not see and that is the test we have to pass in order to control our senses with reason and enjoy the present moment.

It was very complicated for me to understand that we are just one, but from the moment he said that to me in that dream I started wondering if that had been just a dream or if it had been more than one. To say the truth that dream felt so real, it was not like any other dream and I spent much of the day wondering how it was possible. However, the more I wondered the more I confirmed that it was not just any dream. During that week he explained it to me with the graphic. I then had the desire to buy the Bible and the Torah (I already had the Quran) because whenever I went to tell my friends what I was seeing in those unusual dreams some commented "that's in the Bible" and others "that's in the Quran" and even in the Torah.

I felt something inside me that I had to confirm all my dreams and visions because this was not normal, at least not what we categorize as normal. This book was cast as a puzzle with no beginning or end, but it was given simultaneously until it began taking its own form by its own will.

When I was searching for the meaning of Unify, it was an infinite search: It is always one at the end, after counting all the countable numbers, because as many times as you divide it, the result will always be the same, independent of whatever number you choose to be. Mathematically speaking, supposing you are or choose to be the number 5 and you want to divide it by itself, you continue being one. In other words, when you look at another you are looking at a reflection of yourself and as much as we try to multiply within ourselves, we remain one. For example, when you put a mirror in front of a cat, he sees a different cat and he fights with what he sees, not knowing that the other cat he sees is merely a reflection of himself. At that moment he has let himself be fooled by appearances, only that and thinking who he sees is someone else. In the same way, although you may want to divide yourself from the rest, you are the same.

If you think about it, in the sacred books lays that we were made from one and one; God made two.

But at the same time, He united them as a one for life. Then, our Creator told us to multiply, not to separate ourselves, not even from our Creator because when we do, we feel competitive. We feel like we are better than everyone else and we also feel envy. We also start doing things of our own accord without our Creator because we think we don't need him, but that is when we begin to make mistakes. It is necessary for us to unite in order to learn to live in harmony and for us to know he is always with us so we can know the true purpose of our lives. When I meditated in regards to this, something very strong within me said, I needed to look for the translation of Unify in all the languages. Therefore I did, but at the end of my search, I realized that in many languages it means "one." I continued meditating and once again something very strong within me insisted and said I needed to find the mathematical meaning of **Unify**. I continued with my research; and with one click there was the graphic in which our Creator explained somehow we are one. To many people it's something that speaks to us within ourselves; it's our subconscious, to others it's their inner selves. To me, when I meditate, I feel like it is God speaking to me. Let's not ignore that voice, independent of how you define it, because when God wants to speak with you, you don't need to be a prophet, saint or a holy person.

4 UNIFY GRAPHIC

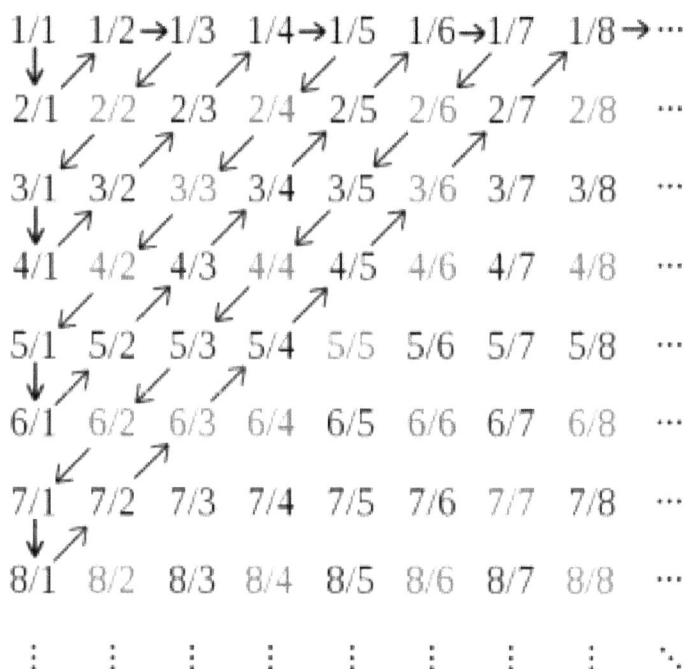

$1/1 \quad 1/2 \rightarrow 1/3 \quad 1/4 \rightarrow 1/5 \quad 1/6 \rightarrow 1/7 \quad 1/8 \rightarrow \cdots$

$2/1 \quad 2/2 \quad 2/3 \quad 2/4 \quad 2/5 \quad 2/6 \quad 2/7 \quad 2/8 \quad \cdots$

$3/1 \quad 3/2 \quad 3/3 \quad 3/4 \quad 3/5 \quad 3/6 \quad 3/7 \quad 3/8 \quad \cdots$

$4/1 \quad 4/2 \quad 4/3 \quad 4/4 \quad 4/5 \quad 4/6 \quad 4/7 \quad 4/8 \quad \cdots$

$5/1 \quad 5/2 \quad 5/3 \quad 5/4 \quad 5/5 \quad 5/6 \quad 5/7 \quad 5/8 \quad \cdots$

$6/1 \quad 6/2 \quad 6/3 \quad 6/4 \quad 6/5 \quad 6/6 \quad 6/7 \quad 6/8 \quad \cdots$

$7/1 \quad 7/2 \quad 7/3 \quad 7/4 \quad 7/5 \quad 7/6 \quad 7/7 \quad 7/8 \quad \cdots$

$8/1 \quad 8/2 \quad 8/3 \quad 8/4 \quad 8/5 \quad 8/6 \quad 8/7 \quad 8/8 \quad \cdots$

$\vdots \qquad \vdots \qquad \vdots \qquad \vdots \qquad \vdots \qquad \vdots \qquad \vdots \qquad \vdots \qquad \ddots$

Cantor is the person in record who presented

the idea of infinite numbers. In the graphic, he is showing us that there is no infinite number, or that no number is bigger than the other. According to his biography, he died shortly before the First World War ended. At that time, all ideas from Georg Cantor sounded crazy, no one believed him because it did not make sense to any of them. His idea was that infinity divided by any number is still infinity, no matter the number. Some people believed him, but others doubted him and thought he was insane. I believe that out of his frustration, being unable to communicate truly what was in his heart, he became depressed. He came to the conclusion that God is the infinite number, but it was difficult to explain and make people understand how we are one, from the first to the last, from the Alpha to the Omega. Even though in his days his ideas sounded crazy they are respected in our time.

I had never heard of Georg Cantor before in my life, but I liked one thing he said. According to those around him, Cantor stated that he had not been the one who invented the ideas about "infinity," but merely someone who had voiced the inner thoughts of God in order to communicate it with the rest of us.

When I read this about Cantor, I could not agree with him more because I had the same feeling. I learned that we are only the discoverers of what is here, created by God for us to uncover. We do not discover many things because we are too busy with our lives, with other things, but when we learn to meditate there is that genius in us that gives us every answer we search for. The bad thing that we do is that we want to own every word, every quote, because we think we are the only ones who have spoken that specific sentence. We want to be asked for permission or to refer to somebody who said it before. However, if we just think, when was ink invented in order to write? I can bet someone said the same phrase a million years ago, but we just don't have the ability to go back in time and really give credit to whoever said it first. I realize that we are not geniuses, but there is a genius in us, the Spirit of our Creator.

In this case I will try to explain this Graphic. What is Unify? Do you understand? It is the expression God used when he created us. He created one right after the other. In other words, Adam was one and of that one he created Eve. Later he told us to multiply, not to divide. Even though now we are many, we will never cease to be one because we are each other's reflection. God's last commandment was, according to the Bible, said by Jesus. It told us to love each other because we were created from one another.

Do you want to believe that you can be one and

the others you? Who is one and the other? It is you on the other side of the mirror. That is why when you see someone who needs help, you should not wait for someone else to do your duty. No one is ever going to do anything, or at least you will stop being one and will be a part of the other, the one that does not care for anything. You will be a part of the one who is always waiting for someone else to do his responsibilities for him. You need to live in the moment so you can help the person who is next to you if they need you.

I was watching the news today and there was a car going up in flames. When the police arrived, they realized there was a lady inside. I noticed there were people around even before the police arrived. My question is, if they were there before the police arrived, why did they wait for the police to come and help and not help the people in the car themselves? Remember, this world is yours and the others', but the other will always be reflected in you. When you see your reflection in another, ask yourself, "Do I like who I really am?" If up to it, your ego will look for excuses, but if not, you don't need them to feel your soul at ease. In this case, instead of judging the other, you will feel compassion for them.

This figure explains how one was taken from

another and how we began to multiply from two into three and how we continued multiplying and reflecting within ourselves, from corner to corner, or however you'd like to call it. From distance to distance, no matter if the distance is short or long between one another; we continue being the same, the reflection of ourselves. Neither the distance nor the color we may have now matters, we will always continue being one. That is why science now knows that we are so alike and that even though we are similar, through DNA we are one. We are unique; there is not one exactly the same as the other. We are one, as he created us from the beginning. Even if we tried to lose ourselves within a crowd, our DNA remains one. We are a part of what needs to come, of what is understanding, of what is unification because we do come from one, created by one, whether we want to believe it or not, whether we understand it or not, only from one. Our Creator, he created everything on this earth from the beginning. And I know that, somehow, there is somewhere for anything that needs to be in order for it to happen.

5 IN MY DREAM

One day, I thought, God of mine what is the earth? Is eternal life here or is it in another place? I was meditating through those questions and I came to understand life is only temporary here, but we are already living the eternal life from here. Picture a snake shedding its skin. We also are leaving our flesh (body) behind, but continue living. I know now that he wants us to follow his wishes in order to lead a life more in order because I realized we are not intelligent enough to lead a life without him. Like many things he left in the holy books, there are many things that don't make sense. 0

Logically, it is hard to believe that unification will take place because we think more of global problems as a political problem and we try to solve them in political terms, with what we already see them. In truth, however, the global problem is not a political problem, but a spiritual one and the solution is in spiritual unification with faith, spirit, and love, not hate or war because we are all like one human family and as a family should do as we believe the best way to solve our problems: with our Creator, with faith, with love, with compassion, with forgiveness, with dedication, with compromise, with loyalty, with perseverance up until the end of our lives so we leave a pattern of life to those who follow us. Not a pattern according to our already confused society, but with our Creator as a guide through everything.

If we base it according to our society, you'll notice they constantly keep changing laws because they are lost. They don't know which ones will work and which won't. This also holds true for medicine and science in general. This is why our bodies and minds are intoxicated with artificial, because we always want to do things with science even do science has been helping in a way to prove many things we thought we could not do before, we had been doing our own laws, not with our Creator.

When I began writing this story, it was such a great impulse that I couldn't even concentrate during my regular job. I knew I needed to write it, but when I made up my mind to do so, I wrote so quickly that in one week I had written 50 pages.

During that time, I had many dreams, but in one of them I was telling our Creator that I needed to know the truth of why my beliefs and truth were contaminated. I didn't know if my truth was the right one. I really felt like I was just an echo formed from everyone, the truth they had formed for them based on what they believed was true, and of others who had lied. It was on that day I had the dream in which we are just a reflection of everyone after having multiplied, but where we continue being one to him.

Now, I understand that we have divided ourselves mentally when we all know we are just the result or total of a multiplication and that we descend from one. Our Creator could have created two, it was not difficult for him to create Eve the same way he created Adam, but if he had, he would have separated us as individuals and we would not have been part of that one until we return to our single Creator. God, you who created us, I asked him, why had you taken so long to speak with us? He responded that he had spoken to all of us many times, in almost every way. He has given us explanations that we know to be true, but refuse to understand.

I asked him why he had taken so long in communicating with us if it was so important. He replied that it was nothing new, that he constantly talked to us, but we ignored him. He told me, "Many times I have sent birds to distract them and teach them how lovely nature is, but even they are ignored along with the nature I have set to make earth beautiful."

That dream was very sad; I woke up crying because I had heard his voice for the very first time. That day I asked him if miracles existed on earth and he told me, "Where do you think it is that all the beautiful things have taken place, those which are spoken of in the holy books?"

I replied, "Here, of course here."

He responded that they keep on occurring, but since we are too preoccupied with too many materialistic things that we tend to ignore them and find logic in them.

Things I could not explain were happening. At that moment I did not know if I was alive, if I was dreaming, if I was insane, or if I was possessed by someone. I asked him to please let me know somehow that it was God who I was talking to. I am not afraid of anything or anybody, but I wanted to make sure those answers were coming from God.

What he told me and made me repeat all night non-stop, I pronounced all night, was that he was our almighty God, our Creator, our Provider and no one could say that except him because everyone, without exception, is afraid of him. I now understood he is the only truth, that what we think we know is only an illusion that remains when our temporary life expires. In other words, what we think is real here, is not. All the steps we take are proof from which we need to walk with firm steps, doing not what we think is correct, but what is correct. If it is not done that way, we ourselves are closing doors with our own hands.

He above sees what one as a person does thinking it is correct. He sees through to what the real intention is of what it may seem to be we are doing. The intention is not chosen by us because many times we try to fool other people and even ourselves of what is the intention with which we do things. However, he knows our minds; he knows if our intentions are others, when we are trying to imply differently, he knows the truth of our hearts. What I understood after writing this paragraph is: Let's not try and negotiate with him, to try and convince him of something he knows for sure, of what the true intention is and try and make him think it is another because we will lose.

The only way we can grow with him is with upfront honesty, with truth, nothing but the truth.

6 LIFE'S PURPOSE

Recently, I realized that we are all meant to be. We have within us along with the reason for who we are, without errors, all to God's perfection. We have everything we have in order to be who we want to be for everything or for no reason. If we don't expand and we don't use the talent we have, then we will have had it for no reason. I watched Nick Vujicic's video, which explains how he found his purpose in life (I really admire this man because he has no legs and no arms. If you want to learn more about him, you can search for him on YouTube.) Although he was not a perfect man in other people's lives he was, in our Creator's eyes, able to discover his purpose in life right in the precise moment he was destined to so he could teach us a life lesson. He discovered that he is an ambassador for God and the message that he is giving us is that he is perfect in the eyes of God for the purpose he was given. His calling was to let us know that realistically speaking, sometimes when we judge ourselves or others we find imperfections, but what we don't know is that in the eyes of God we are perfect for the purpose that we were given. When we find our purpose we will realize that we have everything we need to have in order to be who we need to be, for everything we want to be or for nothing. You may ask yourself, "What do you mean for nothing?" Yes, you may have everything you need for whoever you want to become, but if you don't explore yourself you will never find your calling. God gives you ability for anything you think you are unable to do.

He realized we are a type of gift to serve others with our talents, something unique to us that we can share. If there is a trade of value, if it can be called that, or money for the service we have provided for a job, no matter how little, how much, or if we don't charge for it, no service is ever greater or less than a service obtained by another because the money obtained is only an illusion to our eyes.

We may want to accumulate much money, but we can only spend a certain amount. This is often due to poor health or because we have no time. Even if we have accumulated much money, with which we can buy the best of meals, we no longer can because of our health. On many occasions, the same thing happens; we no longer can enjoy the things we previously desired even if we do have more money.

More or less we are similar to when we discovered the computer, how it has so many benefits, how every part of it has a reason for being there, how we can use it to its limit, in the right sense of the word or using all its benefits in an erroneous way… It was created to benefit everyone with each of its aspects, it has some very good properties and it has a reason for which it exists, but if it was created and not used, stored away, it would not benefit anyone. Or if it is used in a way that will not benefit anyone, it would just go unnoticed with no reason to exist. In other words, you have what it takes to achieve what you want and the thoughts you have are not accidental, they are Divine magic of our creator saying, "Be yourself, because that is why I created you." Just like everything has a reason to exist, you need to discover what is yours.

The Way God May Call You

a) In my experience, I had the urge of finding myself.

b) I had the feeling of being unsatisfied with everything that I had.

c) I had a feeling that there was more than what I was seeing.

d) I had the feeling that nothing, but that mattered. It was as important as taking the next breath of air. Later, when I started meditating, I felt an incomparable joy in my heart, something I had never experienced with anything in my life.

e) I started dreaming the answers to my questions.

f) I started listening in my meditation. It was like somebody was whispering in my ear the answer to every question I asked. It was something like when you are in a classroom and you ask the question, and if you ask the question it is because you don't know the answer. However, the answer was given in a very specific and intelligent way that I could not have answered myself. I was very excited, by asking the questions because the answers were very satisfying. To me, it made complete sense.

AREAS THAT OUR CREATOR MAY HELP US IMPROVE:

1) Without realizing it, we will begin thinking in a different way. We will be less judgmental. In my experience, I was more into judging the moment or at least criticizing what I didn't like about what was happening. I learned to accept the things that each moment brings in a better perspective.

2) We will be more patient. Before, I wanted things instantly, but I learned to be more patient and to learn from every moment, that it is just a moment that is about to change.

3) We will be more loving. Before, because I was seeing things in a different angle, I only used to concentrate in what I did not like about the moment. Now, I learned to love the moment and by doing that, I learned to see the positive way.

4) We will be more faithful. I learned that everything is not up to me because I don't have the capacity to do anything without our Creator. Knowing that he is in me and that he knows my needs just like he knows yours or the needs of anybody else makes me feel fulfilled.

5) We will be more compassionate. Before, I did not know that his Spirit was in everybody. Now that I know that his Spirit is in all of us, and I see someone having a hard time, I feel compassion.

I feel like now that I have learned who our Creator is and where he is, I don't feel lonely anymore. I feel like he is the solution to all my problems. The sooner you surrender to God by allowing him in your life the easier it will be for you.

YOU CAN MAKE A DIFFERENCE AT ANY AGE BECAUSE TIME DOES NOT EXIST

You may feel restricted because of your age,

but you must know time does not exist. When god wants to give you anything time does not matter. Time didn't matter in the example of the lady who was in her 80s and had her first child. That not only happened in the times of the Bible, but it happened recently. If you think it's late, just remember how late it was for Lazarus after four days of being dead.

Don't be afraid if your calling doesn't make sense to others because to whom it needs to make sense to is you. Especially when you know that fulfilling your dreams will make you feel complete and satisfied. Sometimes it will look like you're walking the opposite way from where the others are. In other words, when they run to the left, you're running to the right. As long as you know the right is the way, you should follow your way. Like in the case of Jesus, some people thought he was listening to evil or in the case of Noah, very few people believed him. As long as you know in your heart you're telling the truth to yourself and to the others, it's not up to you to change the perspective of the others because the truth will fall under its own weight.

"The greatest tragedy in life is not death, but life without a purpose." -Myles Munroe.

Many are the plans in a person's heart, but it is the Lord's purpose that prevails. Proverbs 19:21

(NIV)

I was reading the Quran and there was a line that I loved. It was that God is in control over all and every one.

When I learned that, it was easy for me to know that there are no risks involved knowing that if you just trust in any given moment and don't fear, you are on a good path because God is the energy of all.

7 UNIFY

A long time ago, I don't remember exactly how long ago to be honest, perhaps about 20 years, I had a dream. Although it was a very strange dream, it was also a very clear dream. It was so clear that as soon as I awoke, I just had to tell it to my husband. However, in my dream, there had been a word involved in English. At the time I had just begun to learn this language, but my husband did speak it. The word was Unify and my husband, without searching for it in the dictionary, told me it meant something like a union. I told him it could not be because "union" in Spanish was the same word.

The dream caught my attention because I observed that there was a sort of fence surrounding a little fair. Every person that came out from there came out with a different way of thinking. Physically, nothing changed, but I decided to ask one of them something, a woman. We began to speak, but it was not the same way of speaking. I noticed it in the tone of their voice; it was harmonious, peaceful, and tranquil. When I began speaking I understood her look was, caring, and generous, not arrogant. At first sight, I was so curious not only because of what happened with those exiting, but also with the fact that so many people were willing to wait at such a long line to get inside.

In my dream I decided to ask a person I saw exiting, "What is that long line for?" Her response was that in that place everyone was unified. The end of the world was coming and although nobody knew when exactly it would, that is why she had entered. Before it happened, it was necessary for everyone to be unified and that is why she had entered. It was very strange for me to learn it wasn't a religious congregation like there normally is where many people attend, but it was about God. It was something very spiritual, but in the precise moment she finished explaining it to me, I awoke from my dream. I told it to my husband, just like many other dreams I'd had in my life, but I didn't pay much attention. However, that dream was in my mind and from time to time I remembered it, especially when people spoke of the end of the world. I would always think back to that strange dream I had, but it never had much meaning to me. It had been a while, as I mentioned, because I did not have children at the time and in the present time, my first born is 14 years old.

I am sure that there are dreams we all have and just as quickly forget, but there are some that are engraved in our minds and if you think back now you could possibly remember. My belief is I didn't forget this dream because of its astonishing phrases "end of the world" and "unified." During my life I have had many beautiful moments, like when I am hesitant in getting up and almost want to stay living there, but I don't want to talk about myself in this book. Although it is my first, and it is strange, I don't want it to talk about me even though it has to do with me. It is more about God, just like the beginning of our creation.

I have realized recently that after all the experiences I've lived, some beautiful, sad, with hate, resentment, jealousy, some with success and failure, others with selfishness, health, sickness, others with abundance, scarcity, freedom, abstinence, doubt, the majority have been search for faith. At the end of this I have come to the conclusion that they are all stages of life we need to go through. It is necessary to have them otherwise we can't call this life. They are experiences that begin with our thoughts, and then grow with our feelings to attract our negativity, faith, or positivity.

Then we live them, as sequences of events almost like an old film, circling a tape to continue every second, a whole lifetime. Writing a book was always on my mind, but I didn't have an idea to talk about. Everything had been said and talked about and everything was pure logic to everyone. At the same time, it didn't make sense because at this point, everything had already been previously discussed.

I let time pass by without experimenting anything out of the ordinary, nothing that had already been lived or experimented by those who had lived before me. Until recently, the word from my dream came to my mind. This time it was so penetrating that I cannot live without letting the world know because at this moment I feel like it is a necessity we all have regardless of race, religion, social status or age. After all, we are a family. We are the family of Adam and Eve, a dysfunctional family that has been divided by lack of faith, love, and respect. Deep within us this has all been subdivided by us and to this day we continue subdividing ourselves by races and borders. We forget that God created one, a man, and then from his rib, a woman. He created one roof for them, not many or different worlds, however you want to call them. The same is with everything, even the word impossible has been created in our mind. I cannot demand for everyone to believe or stop believing what I write in this book, but it is necessary for you to challenge it. But I think we need to be an army of one to make a difference in this world. I mean if you believe in God and someone is having a hard time somehow in his/her life, you need to let them know they are not alone.

8 THE BIRTH OF JESUS

I ask of our Creator above all things to forgive me if there is something in this book that offends you because after all I'm only one of them that has more questions than answers. However much we want to know, it is him who has the answers to everything. We don't have the ability to change the past when we barely have the ability to live the present. Sometimes when we have a difficult situation in our present we can't even enjoy it. Neither can we predict the future because that only rests in the hands of our Creator.

I have recently been reading all kinds of books from motivational and spiritual books, to both Torah and New Testament of the Bible as well as the Quran. At the moment I know that the more I read, the more I realize how little I know and how I may never finish learning. Within the questions I had for God during my meditation was the one many have asked ourselves regarding religion, and which we all claim to know the answer to. Is Jesus really the son of God? Since everyone claims to know the answer, I took my time to read it in the New Testament of the Bible as well as in the Quran because we have all had that question inside us. When I was reading I found, to my surprise, that it said the same thing, the same exact way the angel Gabriel spoke to Mary, the form by which Mary became pregnant, and how Jesus was born. Not only that, but at this point I wondered how this could all be possible. If what is said in the Quran is the same thing as what is said in the Bible, and both are holy books of God, why would they have this contrast?

After reading all this, my question was stronger than ever because people contradict each other and disagree on one thing or another, yet both books say the exact same thing. I asked God to please explain it to me because when I asked people of each religion, their answers were different, but neither satisfied me. Then one morning I asked God, through meditation, to give me a message. Lately, I had been reading the Bible, the Quran, and the Torah knowing in my heart that there are more books of God, with the intention of finding and understanding everything for my own benefit because I know there are many people who say the Bible was altered when it was translated. In my opinion, I ask how we can know what parts they were. If we don't take the time to investigate it ourselves instead of waiting for the others to do it for us, like with everything else then how can we know who is right and who isn't? In the Quran, it is written that we need to read for ourselves in order to gain wisdom. It is also said the Torah and the Bible are holy books, like the Quran, and that each was written at the moment our creator decided it because everything that happens here, happens by his will. Even the leaf of a tree falls at the right moment. Even though this specific phrase is not in the Bible, there are other ones where it explains that God is in control of everything at every given moment.

In a certain part of the Quran, it clearly specifies in Surah 12 Jose Number 111 that the Quran is not an invented tale, but a corroboration of the previous books and the explanation of all the commandments. It is a guide and mercy for the believers. That day I opened it and in the Quran was the answer to why the Muslims have had controversy for years. If you look for it, in the introduction to Surah 3 Ali Irman (The Family of Irman) in the Quran, Number 59 regarding the case (of the birth) of Jesus is, to God, similar to that of Adam, who was created from the earth. Then he ordered him to, so, he left. Now, the controversy is because I think everyone is right and at the same time is not; it depends on how it is perceived. In the Quran, the reason why our Creator does not consider Jesus or any of us his children, I think, is because we are his creation. As a creation, the love he has for us is much bigger than the love of a father. It is not a comparison between apples and apples because his love is limitless, while as parents, although we may say we adore them, we let them down many times and He has never failed us.

We are the ones who fail by torturing ourselves and not trusting him because we, undoubtedly, belong to him. It does not matter where we stand, who we are, if we believe, if we trust in him, or not, indiscriminately. Let's put it this way, if the Quran and the Bible are written the exact same way in detail, why are they perceived differently? For a moment meditate and think. I do not ask you to agree with me or believe it, it doesn't make sense for me to do so, since after all, I am not writing this book to be right. That is not the purpose of this book because it is not only about me, but about how I am a part of him. The purpose of this book is for you to discover your connection with God from where you are standing so you can see that unity from the beginning, when our surroundings were created. Just as stated in all the holy books, the Torah, the Bible, and the Quran, if Jesus had said Joseph was his father when the Jews asked him, Jesus would have lied. That would not have been true because Mary was not intimate with Joseph in a way to have been impregnated by him. Now think of the response of Jesus, if he had said someone else was his father, of anyone he had named, it would have also been a lie. According to the New Testament, in the Bible, his answer was: God almighty, the Father of all, the Creator of all. That was his truth of how he was created, by the works of the Holy Spirit.

For us humans, everything should be logical in order to make sense. For example, every child must have a father and a mother. Why don't we think about how God created Adam? God created Adam without a father or mother. That means Adam is an orphan, God created him from clay and with a breath gave him life. He said dust you are and dust you will be. In this case, who are Adam's parents? God can do as he wishes with his world, why? Simply, it is because he has the power and not us, just like God was able to create a woman from a man. How can someone be born from a man (Eve from Adam) and what's more illogical, from a rib. It does not make sense. As we all know through the Bible and the Quran, God did not come to this world and have intimacy with Mary, he just asked it be done at that moment in Mary's womb and so it was, the location of it being the only difference. In other words, Jesus is not his son like you are to your father, but yes, we are all the children of God, we are his creation by spirit because our Creator has given us life with it.

We can make a comparison of a relationship between a father and children because for humans, there is no other closer example of unconditional love. No matter how big our love for our children is, not caring about how they are, there will never really be a love as great as the one our Creator has for us. We as parents can fail our children, but although our Creator's love has no limits there are still occasions during which we can't understand why we go through pains. We always think for our benefit that the commandments were given to do our Creator a favor and that is the most certain proof of our lack of reason. Those commandments were actually made so that we would not hurt each other because this is only a participation of life and if we follow them we can live Heaven on earth. We are living a life that in which the spirit has bonded with a body, but the real life is light. That life is in each body from the birth of Adam to the last child that is being born at this moment.

We are brothers by creation, in a bond of love. God is in our veins just like electricity works, going through a device through every corner giving it life, but the battery only has life for so long. If that battery was uncharged, the device would not work and that is why often times we compare ourselves to an electronic saying things like "My battery is low" or "I have no energy." At the end we come back to the same point: We are his creation.

Why do we call each other brothers when we belong to the same congregation? Because we are brothers by creation and we feel we love our Creator with the same love as the other in the same congregation. We know we are not directly brothers by blood, but in spirit because we love him by our own will. Because the love we feel is from the deepest place in our heart, it cannot be bought or lent. It really is unconditional love, pure, without barriers or limits.

Here, my question for you is why did God decide to send Jesus in this way, similarly, but not in the same way he did with Adam? Think about it. God does not improvise or make mistakes; everything he does has a purpose. God knows us individually and knows we are ones that need to see in order to believe, not ones who believe in order to see the way he wishes we were. He wishes we had faith at all times and thought the contrary of what we believe, without trying to find logic in the situation or problem we have. For him, everything is possible and he does not need logic.

When we try to find it in something, we are speaking of what is in our own reach and not of the powers God has, which is why nothing makes sense to us. For that same reason, we do not believe in miracles because miracles are illogical to us using logic or just looking through our eyes, realistically speaking of the form through which we all perceive things. In the Quran it says, similarly, but not the same, that would have made the difference to how we perceived everything. If Jesus had been sent by God and just appeared among us all, a naked man out of nowhere, our Creator would know we would have said, "What is this immoral, naked man doing on the street? Look at that man, has he no shame?" We would have called the available authorities at the time to take him away for being indecent and even crazy. No one would have believed anything he said since there would be no witnesses.

Now, if God had put him in a basket as a baby in the middle of a market or in front of a house, the first thing we would have thought because of our logic would be "What an inconsiderate mother, leaving her child here." Even worse, the child could have been left on the streets without blankets and the people would have been even more disconcerted and angered saying

"That woman is worse than an animal. She didn't even put a scrap of clothe to cover that child."

If we continue thinking with the same logic, if God had sent Jesus to a woman without giving her a divine signal, like the mother of the Prophet Mohammed for example or another woman who already had children at home with a husband, no one would have believed her. Far less would it have been believed since we always give credit of miracles to men.

As I was writing this paragraph regarding Jesus, I had dreams and I meditated in respect to them, accomplishing the ability to decipher them. Personally, they were very clear and they said God, our Creator, was one whether we wanted to believe it or not. I also understood that when he created Jesus, he was and lived in him, just as he lives in our lives. That is why he is the light, the life he gives us is light, a light in a way because in reality there is no way to describe it. We could not move a finger without it. We do not need to be his partner in order for him to take possession of our bodies, no permission or authorization. He can move or keep our bodies from doing so because when he says "this is what shall be done" he is giving an order, not asking for consent. If this were not true, what would be the explanation to Jesus being a baby in the arms of Mary when everyone was questioning her of who was the father of the baby she had in her arms and him telling people who he was, himself. Mary had not been allowed to explain who the father of the baby was.

When I was reading the Bible, I noticed that people were asking Jesus all the time about who his father was. At the same time they were guessing while they asked him, but he was not answering that question. The response was: That was not important at the time, the only thing that mattered was the message he was giving. The whole time Jesus spent here was to help us understand that there was one God and to believe in his name because everything was possible with him, but not without him. This is why Jesus repeated all the time that he could heal anyone, but not to tell anyone what they saw. Why? He wanted to let us know that without God he was nothing and that God was in him, in spirit of life, and in light. That is the reason he was able to produce the miracles he did, because our Creator lives in all of us and in our thoughts. Not only that, but he knows our intentions even before we know them ourselves. In other words, he knows us better than we know ourselves.

What we need to understand is that he created everything we need and at the same time everything was already made, but it is covered and what we need to do is discover it. We need to discover it, but not invent it. We have the tendency to think we are inventors, that we are geniuses. Many times we think we are intelligent, even more than him, but the correct word to call ourselves instead of geniuses is discoverers because what our Creator wants us to do is to discover. All he does is put in our minds what, how, and when. Only when we understand this will we know that there is no way of fooling him because to him we are a glass of clear water and although to us a small speck of dirt is not visible, it is to him.

My answer is that we always give credit to the one who is doing the healing, whether he is a doctor with faith in God or not. If the patient at that moment trusted in God and asked him to help him heal, then he would heal. Jesus was able to heal people because God was with him. To heal one or the other did not matter at that moment. The people he healed at that time are no more special than you and I today. What mattered at the time was the message that he was giving. People these days believe God will heal some people and not the other; the reason why one gets healed and not the other is that one had faith and the other didn't.

God is even in the corners where our sight cannot reach, but we always try to find logic in it. We spend our time calling miracles coincidences. We need to see in order to believe up until now. We always need a logical comment for everything. I think this is the reason why we don't know what to believe these days: we are constantly trying to find logic in everything we see. This is why we commit errors and why we watch others commit the same ones again. Because of logic, we have accepted it, thinking that because our neighbor has done something it is now acceptable for us to do it. Our creator left us rules to follow in his Holy Books, which he made despite him already giving us the gift of reason. However, he left those books in case our reasoning still does not take charge, and he loves us despite what we do, so we won't hurt each other. He also gave us emotions so we know when we need to correct our mistakes. For example, when we are happy we know there is nothing to be set right. When we feel like heroes it is because we have done a good deed in some way. However, when we have done something bad we feel like we have to lie because we don't want anyone to know it and we feel guilty. These are the alerts in our soul telling us to change that because it's not right and therefore we cannot live with faith. Meanwhile, we miss the message Jesus and the other Prophets have brought us.

Said message is for us to love one another like God loves us. The biggest thing in all religion, without exception, is that we are taught to put our Creator above all other things. In other words, we must put him before anything and anyone else, even ourselves. Even though our Creator told us we need to respect our parents, we need to put our Creator before them as well. Another question I had was: If God wants us to honor our parents, why would we need to put our Creator before them?

The answer was that many times as parents we have many flaws, due to our weaknesses, and our own children can see them. Here is an example. Let's say your father plans to rob a bank and asks you to help him. If you put God over all, you will know that is the wrong thing to do and will not help him. We need to put our Creator before everything and we need to show our children to follow our Creator's guide. When we put our Creator first we'll know who the priority in our life is and what the right thing to do is. If we do this during the test of our lives you'll understand who you are really serving –God or your ego.

Sometimes, it is easier to focus on something to distract ourselves from what we are doing and keep us thinking we are always right whether it be because we are the parents or we have a higher education level. As I often hear it, if we have our own beliefs and our children don't share them, they will not be saved. I am sure the act of love we should give them is with the purpose of them getting saved along with us. After all, we are all on the same boat. We are not thinking of the purpose for which God sent Jesus, but the form in which he did since it is the way we wanted to see it. However, whatever the form, it does not change the fact of what happened. God wanted something to happen and so it did because he is God and he can do as he wishes, however he wishes.

A similar situation is that of the glass of water. Now, my question is this: What do you think of the glass?

Some will tell me the glass is half full, but others will tell me it is half empty.

This will not change the fact that it is a cup containing a certain amount of water and that the "emptiness" is filled with energy or as some people may call it, oxygen.

Let's focus on the purpose of God sending Jesus to share his messages with us. What was the intention of God? What did he say? What did he do when he met with those who did not believe in God? Jesus did not say "I'm saved. They can save themselves, if they want. It's their problem if they don't believe it." Quite the contrary, Jesus in many ways was teaching us that each miracle he performed had a purpose. It was to revive our faith, just like when he asked Lazarus to wake up from the tomb after four days of being dead.

Sometimes I hear people ask themselves when the end of the world will be. Even I asked myself that question, but if you think about it logically, there must be a reason why God told no one the date or time of the end of the world because he does know it.

When I have meditated regarding this subject in particular, I have asked my subconscious or our Creator and the answer is: It will not matter when it will happen, the important thing is the end of the world you have created for yourself because all accounts are individual. Most religions call this the Judgment Day.

I have been reading the Torah and Psalms 144.14 asks what should be the worries of the men. The answer was that our lives here are like a breath of life and our days are like a passing shadow.

Are you waiting for a sign to start being good to yourself and to others, to connect by faith with him? Have you not thought that your body will expire before that day that is talked about so much? You won't have time to repent, not even to prepare to be in that place that is talked about so often. Like Buddha said, "Holding onto anger is like drinking poison and expecting the other person to die."

That is why it is not necessary to believe everything said without taking the time to search for it by your own account, to read for your own benefit and everyone else's. Thinking about helping and salvation may save you even from your enemy, not with wars, but with love.

Why don't we analyze this: If I ask you about your grandparents, will you be able to tell me about what happened during their lives in detail? Perhaps you will know a part of what happened because you heard it through your parents, but not as detailed as we do when we speak to the maximum with dates and exact words. With the same intention, I ask you:

In the recent argument you had with your father, your spouse, your brother or son, do you remember what you said, word for word? You could tell me something close to what you expressed at that moment, but not the intentions of what you said. Even if that is how things happened, it was because of what you thought at that moment, but at the current moment you have thought of other things and perhaps you may not think the way you did back then.

We are always in a constant battle to prove to the world that we are right and that we are the ones saying the truth while the rest of us are wrong. We often forget that the sole idea that we must always be right has divided us as partners in matrimony, as family, as a nation, and, finally, as the unanimous form from which we began, one for all and all for one. As we waste time trying to change history and being right, there are others who are dying of hunger or of pain because they don't have what others have plenty of out of selfishness. This is why when you have the opportunity to help someone, you should do it, but it is better if the person is a stranger. This way, you don't expect payment for it later; otherwise the intention for helping would not have been what it should. We should help simply because it is our duty. Whenever you donate something, make sure it gets to the person who is in need and is benefited by it. If you help someway, do it from your heart. If you expect some kind of reward it is better to decline because everything you do, good or bad, will be accumulated in your personal account.

I have another question for you regarding the human law. Do you think it is fair if your brother kills someone or causes a problem and you are the one who pays for the crime? Is it fair if you are the one who is imprisoned or worse? Is it fair for you to take his place? Logically, the answer is no because we know we act as individuals and our thoughts and emotions are separate. Therefore, you shouldn't have to pay for something your parents or grandparents did, it is irrelevant. Right now it is your time to experiment what they did during their time and now you have other ideas.

The point to all of this is: why are we emphasized who killed who or who did wrong in the Bible, Quran, or Torah in those times? No matter how much we would like to, we cannot change the difficult or good moments that have existed during which people have acted irrationally, then or now. If we analyze it further, there have always existed people with bad intentions, then and now, in all the religions, and much more within people who don't follow a religion. Let's let the stories that have happened remain that way and not try to reinvent them. It is alright to use them as a reference and guide to differentiate between right and wrong, but accepting it as something past and respecting it. Not to justify our wrongs because we are always taking references of something similar to our situation and saying "If this person committed this injustice or mistake, why can't I?"

For unification, it is important to live individually, knowing our personal accounts are just those, unique. It is not about your relationship with someone else, it is about your relationship with our Creator. The current wars have no reason to exist. If you analyze them, they are not for God; they began because people want to be right. The worst part is that if you ask each one of them, they all think they are correct and their belief is so strong they are willing to die for it.

I have found in all the holy books that God wanted us to love one another as much as we love ourselves, without exceptions. He did not say to exclude our enemies or that if we are cooking something and our neighbor smells it, we should share with them. Before we judge someone, we have to look at ourselves. In fact, it clearly says this is not our actual life, that there is eternal life. Religiously, the holy books are considered to be a guide or manual of how to live life, but like always, we believe we know it all. A clearer example is when we buy something new that includes instructions. Usually, we push the instructions aside and try to set it up or build whatever it is using our logic. We often do make our purchases work; however, we often miss out on other features or benefits we could have gained by reading the instructions. We turn to the instructions only when we realize something is not functioning correctly in order to find our errors and make it work.

My question is: If there are so many instruction manuals in the world, of everything and for everything, why don't we look for them, even if we need them? Sometimes we do, other times we don't and we remain frustrated. Those books are in us. How was God able to make a woman from a man? How can someone be born from a man? Even more illogically: from a rib? It is illogical, it does not make sense. We keep trying to find sense in it and we keep making the same mistakes over and over again. Another example is that sometimes we believe in horoscopes we read and we believe that person even though we have no idea where they got all of it from. It is according to her imagination that she says things supposedly based on the day or the month you were born. Yet, you believe it and sometimes you go as far as to have someone read your palm.

Do you really believe them? If you really do, ask them one question: Who is our Creator? Who created them and those around them? They will tell you it was God Almighty, our Creator. If they believe it, why don't you? Why don't you believe he has absolute power, power to help you with whatever you need? He, with his infinite light, can give you all that you need. You can live the life you want, within yourself, not the life others want you to live. Of course this is all possible, but within its own rules, submitting to your wishes. One moment you'll think you can do it all because you are or have all you want and you don't need him.

It's at the moment when he leaves you and you lose yourself within. If you believe you have all the power to live your life happily without him, why don't you test it out? Go to the beach and try to make a sculpture of a man, out of sand, like our creator did. Try to give it life. If you are a good builder, you may make him perfectly, but only that far. You will never be able to give it life; Jesus was able to do it with God's will.

That was his teaching, that we are a zero on the left. We do not matter, we do not create, we have no will, we are nothing compared to him. Even using a mathematic graph, depending on where you place the zero is if it matters or not. When it is on the right side it matters, but on the left side it does not. You are either with God or you are not, there is no neutral side for a zero. With him you are everything, without him you are nothing. Like in the case of Michael Jackson, he had everything he wanted and thought hiring a personal medic just for himself would buy him care 24 hours a day.

I have understood that he patented the discovery of an anti-gravity shoe design for his shoes in 1993. Where is that fortune? Where are all his achievements? Where is he? To all those who blindly believe in science only and not in God, they are so behind that they are finding a way to freeze a body in order to melt it and bring it back to life later so it will live forever. I want to share this report with you. Everything that is in this world has been permitted by God. Science is to prove to ourselves how everything works in its natural way. Science is not all, and men are not really in control of science even though in a way it may look like it. God is always in control of everything, even of science. God gives science what they need to know. Everything that he created is doing what it's supposed to be doing in their natural way.

9 SCIENCE TRYING TO DISCOVER ETERNAL LIFE

I say discover because eternal life is already there for the ones who already discovered it. For the ones who think life is limited to the body, practically dying is hell, as described in the Bible.

"I give them eternal life, and they will never perish, and no one will snatch them out of my hand." John 10:28

Jesus was very specific about how he referred to what dying is. He described that dying is sleeping, in a way. He showed that the Spirit of God can wake up the body even after four days of having died, in our perspective of what dying is. He was so confident that dying is not what we think it is that when Jesus was preaching the word of God, a man came up to him and told him that he would like to follow Jesus, but that his father had just passed away and he wanted to bury his father first before going with him. Jesus was not sarcastic, but he wanted to make sure we understood what dying is. In Luke 9:60 Jesus said to that man "Let the dead bury their own dead, but you go and proclaim the kingdom of God."

The Kingdom of God is believing that dying doesn't exist. The Kingdom of God would be like Jesus said in Matthew 10:28, "And do not fear those who kill the body but cannot kill the soul. Rather fear him who can destroy both soul and body in hell." Believing that you are going to die and never be alive again is unaccepted by your soul because your soul knows and believes in the eternal life. When you think about dying and never being alive again, dying, as well as living in fear, is hell for your spirit. the Bible, the Quran, and the Torah talk about hell. The Quran says that the definition of hell is warning. According to the Bible, hell is dying, but when they talk about dying, they are talking about death of the Spirit, not the body. Hell is living in condemnation because your spirit is not alive, it is not at ease. In the Torah, it says "For they are like a breath of air; their days are like a passing shadow." Psalm 144:4. In a way it is encouraging everyone to live and enjoy the present time.

Science, based on what science fiction writers predicted about humanity conquering death, is working on developing possible forms of reaching immortality. A few examples of their contemplations are cloning, cultivation of stem cells, nanotechnology, and cryonics. For those who have not heard of cryonics, it is a technique of deep-freezing the bodies of those who have died of an incurable disease, in the hope of a future cure.

There are companies already offering this service, throughout the world. Their current plan is to freeze the person's body and brain until they figure out how to make them immortal. They believe that the essence of a person is in their brain. The prices to preserve the body and brain vary from country to country, starting at $10,000 to $80,000 for a head and $30,000 to $150,000 for an entire body.

They have frozen at least 150 bodies, making them believe they figured out how to make the body immortal. Meditating in regards to this subject, I believe that what is happening with anybody who doesn't believe in the eternal life is that they are looking for the eternal life in the external, not in the spirit. Once you learn to meditate, and you learn to find yourself internally, you will find the answer yourself of the eternal life. Never try to find yourself in the opinion of others because the moment you do that you are allowing for anybody to kill the spirit of your life. No one and nothing can kill the Spirit of Life given by God. Accepting this is accepting eternal life.

When I was meditating on this study by scientists, I had a question for our creator. (Knowing that with God all things are possible but without our Creator nothing is possible.) My question was: God, are you going to allow this person to give life after death, as you allowed Jesus?

The answer was in meditation during a dream (the form through which most of my answers have come.) In my dream he said he always sees the intention of everything we do, say, and think. *What is the intention of everyone?* He told me to ask the scientists if they could freeze light. Our soul has the Spirit of Life and he gives us that life through light. He said while that body has life, they can do whatever they wish with it, but once it was dead they no longer could. That was because our body is just a costume made for our soul and our spirit is the light that gives it life.

God decides to give or take the light of life;

only he can possess that authorization. In that dream he told me through meditation that he wanted me to know how the soul and spirit live in diverse situations. The way we humans die, or our bodies do, is just a decision of God, our Creator. He explained in that moment the different forms by which we die, like if a body was drowned.

Can science drown light? Can they submerge it and destroy it? Ask them that.

He continued. *Can they burn light like a body dies when it is burnt? Ask them.*

Ask them if they can freeze the soul and spirit along with the body without my authorization. Can they freeze light like a body when it dies frozen? They could freeze the body, but without the soul or spirit because they are simply light.

To end this explanation in full, they cannot destroy light. They cannot cut it, kill it, or make it explode. If there is a ray of light, as minute as it may be, perhaps they can shield themselves from it, but nothing more.

He always sees the intention of which we are trying to find out anything that comes to our mind. If someone thinks they don't need God to do any experiments or think they can reinvent man, it is impossible. You cannot invent something that is already there. It's not possible in the way they are searching. Like Wayne Dyer says, you lost your key to your house and your house is dark, but you are looking for the key outside on the street because there is light outside. You will never find your key outside because the key is not outside, it is inside your house.

In this case, they could only give eternal life to those who could afford it, doing it for the money. Leaving the poor without eternal life would not be fair, would it? That is why God will not allow eternal life to be given this way. We are not good judges, fair or just. That is why they do not want to believe he is the only one who can give eternal life. However, eternal life is for everyone because there is no death.

10 UNDERSTANDING I AM THAT I AM

Psalm 75
*We give you thanks, O God, we give you thanks, ***
calling upon your Name and declaring all your
wonderful deeds.

I realized that sometimes we want to know everything, but we want to find a shortcut and when we do that, we miss a lot of things. In the case of Jesus, when I used to read "I am the Truth, I am the Way, and I am the Life" I did not realize that I needed to learn more about the word "I Am."

The first time I read the verses in regards to Jesus saying "I am the Truth, I am the Way, and I am the life" and "[57]So the Jews said to Him, "You are not yet fifty years old, and have You seen Abraham?"

[58]Jesus said to them, "Truly, truly, I say to you, before Abraham was born, I am." I honestly got confused. I thought he meant that he was the God. However, I didn't know the meaning of "I Am" in the Old Testament when God explained to Moses that his name was "I Am" and that that will be his name forever. Abraham was born before Jesus, but when they asked Jesus "You are not yet fifty years old and have you seen Abraham?" that question was made because the Jews were misunderstanding him as well when he said "I am before Abraham." What he meant to say was that God was before Abraham. If he wanted to say that he was born before Abraham he would have said it. The way he would have said it would have been "I was born before Abraham was born" or "I was here before Abraham." We need to pay attention to what he really said to be able to understand him.

When I was able to read The Quran and I had questions in regards to Jesus, Prophet Muhammad made me realize I needed to follow the steps of Jesus, in the Bible, just like he says "I am the way." When I did this I realized with Jesus's words that the definition of dying was not dying. That is how I found out about the eternal life. When I read a little bit more and tried to understand what Jesus was saying about the eternal life, I realized hell is dying. I found out about the truth through Jesus and the sentence "I am that I am" because when I went back to Moses, Jesus said "I am that I am" was before Abraham. When I read about Moses I realized that Moses was the one who heard, according to what we know, the name of God for the first time: "I am that I am."

Abraham was before Moses, and in his time nobody knew the name of God. If we could describe God, it would be that he is a Spirit. I want to share with you this part of the Quran, the Bible, and the Torah as proof of everything that I am saying. You will find the following verse in repetition, but I wanted to show that you will find the same thing in all the Bible versions. I only did it in these verses because I wanted to make sure you knew it was the same, as well as with everything else that I have quoted from the Bible. I wanted you to know that all the parts may be slightly different, but they all mean the same thing.

Verses of Exodus 3:14
New International Version
God said to Moses, "I AM WHO I AM. This is what you are to say to the Israelites: 'I AM has sent me to you.'"

New Living Translation
God replied to Moses, "I Am Who I Am. Say this to the people of Israel: I Am has sent me to you."

English Standard Version
God said to Moses, "I AM WHO I AM." And he said, "Say this to the people of Israel, 'I AM has sent me to you.'"

New American Standard Bible
God said to Moses, "I AM WHO I AM"; and He said, "Thus you shall say to the sons of Israel, 'I AM has sent me to you.'"

King James Bible
and God said unto Moses, I AM THAT I AM: and he said, Thus shalt thou say unto the children of Israel, I AM hath sent me unto you.

Holman Christian Standard Bible
God replied to Moses, "I AM WHO I AM. This is what you are to say to the Israelites: I AM has sent me to you."

International Standard Version
God replied to Moses, "I AM WHO I AM," and then said, "Tell the Israelis: 'I AM sent me to you.'"

NET Bible
God said to Moses, "I am that I am." And he said, "You must say this to the Israelites, 'I am has sent me to you.'"

GOD'S WORD® Translation
God answered Moses, "I Am Who I Am. This is what
you must say to the people of Israel: 'I Am has sent me
to you.'"

Jubilee Bible 2000
And God answered unto Moses, I AM THAT I AM. And
he said, Thus shalt thou say unto the sons of Israel: I
AM (YHWH) has sent me unto you.

King James 2000 Bible
And God said unto Moses, I AM THAT I AM: and he
said, Thus shall you say unto the
Children of Israel, I AM has sent me unto you.

American King James Version
and God said to Moses, I AM THAT I AM: and he said,
Thus shall you say to the children of Israel, I AM has
sent me to you.

American Standard Version
and God said unto Moses, I AM THAT I AM: and he
said, Thus shalt thou say unto the children of Israel, I
AM hath sent me unto you.

Douay-Rheims Bible
God said to Moses: I AM WHO AM. He said: Thus
shalt thou say to the children of Israel: HE WHO IS

hath sent me to you.

Darby Bible Translation
and God said to Moses, I AM THAT I AM. And he said,
Thus shalt thou say unto the children of Israel: I AM
hath sent me unto you.

English Revised Version
And God said unto Moses, I AM THAT I AM: and he
said, Thus shalt thou say unto the children of Israel, I
AM hath sent me unto you.

Webster's Bible Translation
and God said to Moses, I AM THAT I AM: And he
said, Thus shalt thou say to the children of Israel, I AM
hath sent me to you.

World English Bible
God said to Moses, "I AM WHO I AM," and he said,
"You shall tell the children of Israel this: 'I AM has
sent me to you.'"

Young's Literal Translation
And God saith unto Moses, 'I AM THAT WHICH I
AM;' He saith also, 'Thus dost thou say to the sons of
Israel, I AM hath sent me unto you.'

Jubilee Bible 2000

And God answered unto Moses, I AM THAT I AM. And he said, Thus shalt thou say unto the sons of Israel: I AM (YHWH) has sent me unto you.

King James 2000 Bible
And God said unto Moses, I AM THAT I AM: and he said, Thus shall you say unto the and forever. 3. That he is incomprehensible; we cannot by searching find him out: this name checks all bold and curious inquiries concerning God. 4. That he is faithful and true to all his promises, unchangeable in his word as well as in his nature; let Israel know this, I AM hath sent me unto you. I am, and there is none else besides me. All else have their being from God, and are wholly dependent upon him. Also, here is a name that denotes what God is to his people. The Lord God of your fathers sent me unto you. Moses must revive among them the religion of their fathers, which was almost lost; and then they might expect the speedy performance of the promises made unto their fathers.

Moses   at   the   Burning   Bush
*   ...13Then Moses said to God, "Behold, I am going to the sons of Israel, and I will say to them, 'The God of your fathers has sent me to you.' Now they may say to me, 'What is His name?' What shall I say to them?" 14God said to Moses, "I AM WHO I AM"; and He said, "Thus you shall say to the sons of Israel, 'I*

AM has sent me to you.'" 15God, furthermore, said to Moses, "Thus you shall say to the sons of Israel, 'The LORD, the God of your fathers

I am that I am **Exodus 3:15**
The God of Abraham, the God of Isaac, and the God of Jacob, has sent me to you.' This is my name forever, and this is my memorial-name to all generations....
Cross References
John 8:24
I told you that you would die in your sins; if you do not believe that I am he, you will indeed die in your sins."

John 8:28
So Jesus said, "When you have lifted up the Son of Man, then you will know that I am he and that I do nothing on my own but speak just what the Father has taught me.

John 8:58
"Very truly I tell you," Jesus answered, "before Abraham was born, I am

Hebrews 13:8
Jesus Christ is the same yesterday and today and forever.

(Jesus was not lying, Jesus was Jesus then, Jesus is

Jesus now, and he will be forever. God was God from day 1 and is God now and forever. The sea will be the sea now and forever. The air is the air today, now and forever. I was born to be me and I will not stop being me and I will be who I am even after I am no longer here for the people who will remember me.)

Revelation 1:8
"I am the Alpha and the Omega," says the Lord God, "who is, and who was, and who is to come, the Almighty."

Revelation 4:8
Each of the four living creatures had six wings and was covered with eyes all around, even under its wings. Day and night they never stop saying: "'Holy, holy, holy is the Lord God Almighty,' who was, and is, and is to come."

The 99 Names of God in the Quran
These are the names of God. Just picture God telling you all this with the words "I am" before the 99 names, Like God telling you who he is to you:

Asma al-Husna - The Most Beautiful Names of God - the 99 Names Of Allah. Read the translation of the 99 Names of Allah in the following table.

English translation of 99 names of Allah
Asmaa'u Allah Al-Hosna
أسماء الله الحسنى

الل	I am The Greatest Name	Allah
الرحمن	I am The All-Compassionate	Ar-Rahman
الرحيم	I am The All-Merciful	Ar-Rahim
الملك	I am The Absolute Ruler	Al-Malik
القدوس	I am The Pure One	Al-Quddus
السلام	I am The Source of Peace	As-Salam
المؤمن	I am The Inspirer of Faith	Al-Mu'min
المهيمن	I am The Guardian	Al-Muhaymin
العزيز	I am The Victorious	Al-Aziz
الجبار	I am The Compeller	Al-Jabbar
المتكبر	I am The Greatest	Al Mutakabbir
الخالق	I am The Creator	Al-Khaliq
البارئ	I am The Maker of Order	Al-Bari'
المصور	I am The Shaper of Beauty	Al-Musawwir
الغفار	I am The Forgiving	Al-Ghaffar
القهار	I am The Subduer	Al-Qahhar
الوهاب	I am The Giver of All	Al-Wahhab
الرزاق	I am The Sustainer	Ar-Razzaq
الفتاح	I am The Opener	Al-Fattah
العليم	I am The Knower of All	Al-`Alim
القابض	I am The Constrictor	Al-Qabid
الباسط	I am The Reliever	Al-Basit
الخافض	I am The Abaser	Al-Khafid
الرافع	I am The Exalter	Ar-Rafi
المعز	I am The Bestower of Honors	Al-Mu'izz
المذل	I am The Humiliator	Al-Mudhill

السميع	I am The Hearer of All	As-Sami
البصير	I am The Seer of All	Al-Basir
الحكم	I am The Judge	Al-Hakam
العدل	I am The Just	Al-`Adl
اللطيف	I am The Subtle One	Al-Latif
الخبير	I am The All-Aware	Al-Khabir
الحليم	I am The Forbearing	Al-Halim
العظيم	I am The Magnificent	Al-Azim
الغفور	I am The Forgiver and Hider of Faults	Al-Ghafur
الشكور	I am The Rewarder of Thankfulness	Ash-Shakur
العلي	I am The Highest	Al-Ali
الكبير	I am The Greatest	Al-Kabir
الحفيظ	I am The Preserver	Al-Hafiz
المقيت	I am The Nourisher	Al-Muqit
الحسيب	I am The Accouter	Al-Hasib
الجليل	I am The Mighty	Al-Jalil
الكريم	I am The Generous	Al-Karim
الرقيب	I am The Watchful One	Ar-Raqib
المجيب	I am The Responder to Prayer	Al-Mujib
الواسع	I am The All-Comprehending	Al-Wasi
الحكيم	I am The Perfectly Wise	Al-Hakim
الودود	I am The Loving One	Al-Wadud
المجيد	I am The Majestic One	Al-Majid
الباعث	I am The Resurrector	Al-Ba'ith
الشهيد	I am The Witness	Ash-Shahid
الحق	I am The Truth	Al-Haqq
الوكيل	I am The Trustee	Al-Wakil
القوى	I am The Possessor of All Strength	Al-Qawiyy
المتين	I am The Forceful One	Al-Matin
الولي	I am The Governor	Al-Waliyy
الحميد	I am The Praised One	Al-Hamid
المحصى	I am The Appraiser	Al-Muhsi

المبدئ	I am The Originator	Al-Mubdi'
المعيد	I am The Restorer	Al-Mu'id
المحيي	I am The Giver of Life	Al-Muhyi
المميت	I am The Taker of Life	Al-Mumit
الحي	I am The Ever Living One	Al-Hayy
القيوم	I am The Self-Existing One	Al-Qayyum
الواجد	I am The Finder	Al-Wajid
الماجد	I am The Glorious	Al-Majid
الواحد	I am The One, the All Inclusive The Indivisible	Al-Wahid
الصمد	I am The Satisfier of All Needs	As-Samad
القادر	I am The All Powerful	Al-Qadir
المقتدر	I am The Creator of All Power	Al-Muqtadir
المقدم	I am The Expediter	Al-Muqaddim
المؤخر	I am The Delayer	Al-Mu'akhkhir
الأول	I am The First	Al-Awwal
الآخر	I am The Last	Al-Akhir
الظاهر	I am The Manifest One	Az-Zahir
الباطن	I am The Hidden One	Al-Batin
الوالي	I am The Protecting Friend	Al-Wali
المتعال	I am The Supreme One	Al-Muta'ali
البر	I am The Doer of Good	Al-Barr
التواب	I am The Guide to Repentance	At-Tawwab
المنتقم	I am The Avenger	Al-Muntaqim
العفو	I am The Forgiver	Al-'Afuww
الرؤوف	I am The Clement	Ar-Ra'uf
مالك الملك	I am The Owner of All	Malik-al-Mulk
الجلال ذو و الإكرام	I am The Lord of Majesty and Bounty	Dhu-al-Jalal wa-al-Ikram
المقسط	I am The Equitable One	Al-Muqsit
الجامع	I am The Gatherer	Al-Jami'
الغني	I am The Rich One	Al-Ghani
المغني	I am The Enricher	Al-Mughni
المانع	I am The Preventer of Harm	Al-Mani'

الضار	I am The Creator of The Harmful	Ad-Darr
النافع	I am The Creator of Good	An-Nafi'
النور	I am The Light	An-Nur
الهادي	I am The Guide	Al-Hadi
البديع	I am The Originator	Al-Badi
الباقي	I am The Everlasting One	Al-Baqi
الوارث	I am The Inheritor of All	Al-Warith
الرشيد	I am The Righteous Teacher	Ar-Rashid
الصبور	I am The Patient One	As-Sabur

Psalm 46:10 in the Bible.

I was meditating on this word…(be still and know that I am God, I will be exalted among the nations, I will be exalted in the earth,)

In one word, I Am is the only one you need because "What I am not" is fear. God is all we need in our lives.

This is exactly what happens when you meditate. And just stay still when God starts giving you thoughts, inside you, but is not you. If you just learn to listen he will reveal to you anything you need to know, because he is: "I am", God, inside you. Don't get confused, you are not God, because you cannot do anything without him, but when you learn that he is in you, you feel in peace, you feel Unified, you feel protected by him. You really feel like you don't need anything else artificial, like material things. You feel like you don't need to depend on anything but God to be happy because you feel fulfilled. At the same time you will learn to see yourself and the others, therefore. You will learn to understand that he is in the others as well, you will learn to see the other with no judgments because you will know if you judge the other you are only judging yourself, because they are your reflection and you are judging God at the same time because he is in them at the same time he is in you.

Parallel Verses
New International Version
"He says, 'Be still, and know that I am God; I will be exalted among the nations, I will be exalted in the earth.'"

New Living Translation
"Be still, and know that I am God! I will be honored by every nation. I will be honored throughout the world."

English Standard Version
"Be still, and know that I am God. I will be exalted among the nations, I will be exalted in the earth!"

New American Standard Bible
"Cease striving and know that I am God; I will be exalted among the nations, I will be exalted in the earth."

King James Bible

"Be still, and know that I am God: I will be exalted among the heathen, I will be exalted in the earth."

Holman Christian Standard Bible
"Stop your fighting--and know that I am God, exalted among the nations, exalted on the earth."
International Standard Version
"Be in awe and know that I am God. I will be exalted among the nations. I will be exalted throughout the earth."

NET Bible
"He says, 'Stop your striving and recognize that I am God! I will be exalted over the nations! I will be exalted over the earth!'"

Aramaic Bible in Plain English
"Return and know that I AM GOD. I am exalted among the nations and I am exalted in the Earth."

GOD'S WORD® Translation
"Let go [of your concerns]! Then you will know that I am God. I rule the nations. I rule the earth."

Jubilee Bible 2000
"Be still, and know that I am God; I will be exalted in the Gentiles, I will be exalted in the earth."

King James 2000 Bible
"Be still, and know that I am God: I will be exalted
among the nations, I will be exalted in the earth."

American King James Version
"Be still, and know that I am God: I will be exalted
among the heathen, I will be exalted in the earth."

American Standard Version
"Be still, and know that I am God: I will be exalted
among the nations, I will be exalted in the earth."

Douay-Rheims Bible
"Be still and see that I am God; I will be exalted
among the nations, and I will be exalted in the earth."

Darby Bible Translation
"Be still, and know that I am God: I will be exalted
among the nations, I will be exalted in the earth."

English Revised Version
"Be still, and know that I am God: I will be exalted
among the nations, I will be exalted in the earth."
Webster's Bible Translation
"Be still, and know that I am God: I will be exalted
among the heathen, I will be exalted in the earth."

World English Bible

"Be still, and know that I am God. I will be exalted among the nations. I will be exalted in the earth."

Young's Literal Translation
"Desist, and know that I am God, I am exalted among nations, I am exalted in the earth."

Jesus knew this and trusted God. The reason why Jesus was able to do all that he did was because he listened and obeyed God's Spirit.

Impossible   I'm possible

A week ago, I went to a workshop for business and internet. Adam Ginsbergs mentioned about he had a thought in the morning, while he was preparing for his seminar. I asked him if I could use his quote because I understood that very well, now that I know who is and where I Am is. He said, "Impossible is I'm possible, I am possible, when you underline the first two letters in Impossible."

11 JESUS

John 19:26-27
New International Version (NIV)

26 When Jesus saw his mother there, and the disciple whom he loved standing nearby, he said to her, "Woman,[a] here is your son," 27 and to the disciple, "Here is your mother." From that time on, this disciple took her into his home.

I asked God, through my meditation why Jesus said that to John. Why did Jesus not say to John; John here is my mother take care of her, like she is your mother and you, Mother, take care of John like he is your own son.

This is what I received for an answer, because in God we are one.

Jesus's Claims about Himself

48 The Jews answered him, "Aren't we right in saying that you are a Samaritan and demon-possessed?"
49 "I am not possessed by a demon," said Jesus, "but I honor my Father and you dishonor me. 50 I am not seeking glory for myself; but there is one who seeks it, and he is the judge. 51 Very truly I tell you, whoever obeys my word will never see death."
52 At this they exclaimed, "Now we know that you are demon-possessed! Abraham died and so did the prophets, yet you say that whoever obeys your word will never taste death. 53 Are you greater than our father Abraham? He died, and so did the prophets. Who do you think you are?"

That's what Jesus said to the people who questioned who he was because he knew that he was not God:

John 8
54 "Jesus replied, 'If I glorify myself, my glory means nothing. My Father, whom you claim as your God, is the one who glorifies me. 55 Though you do not know him, I know him. If I said I did not, I would be a liar like you, but I do know him and obey his word. 56 Your father Abraham rejoiced at the thought of seeing my day; he saw it and was glad.'"

Jesus never lied, but we misunderstood him.

Jesus needed the Creator and Provider, like all of us. The spirit of God is what made him who he was and all the beautiful things he did, according to our logic.

When I was correcting the book in regards to the topic that Jesus never lied, but we misunderstood him I had a dream. I dreamt that I was correcting the book and in my dream I was meditating. And in my meditation our Creator said to me that by asking Jesus directly for what we wanted, we are denying God or making Jesus, in a way, like Caesar. Because when Caesar found out that we needed to adore one God, Caesar wanted to be the God and he created his statue to be adored. If we think Jesus said that, we need to read again, but this time we need to read in a way like we are hearing from his own lips what he was saying. Because if we are asking Jesus and we think that Jesus is the God, we are making Jesus atheist.

So, we need to hear him when he said to enter from the narrow door. Why did he answer in that way? We must learn to read the Bible, the Quran, and the Torah as if we are seeing a logo. When you see a logo, sometimes they have hidden messages and you can see it from one point of view, but that is actually the big door. When you look in deeper, that is when you can find the true meaning of anything. In the case of the Bible we have to pay attention to what Jesus and Moses said because that is the truth and that is the narrow door, not what the rest of the people were saying – they were just speculating.

Going through the big door is going off of what everyone else thinks, but getting with the truth of God is going in through the narrow door, which will be the ones who received the true message. We normally get lost in the details of everybody's opinion, but that, again, is the big door. That is the door that gets you lost, that according to your logical thinking, is the right path. That is actually the path that ends, in our logical thinking, living in agony – with all the torments and pain from your soul. That is not being alive; it is what they call "the death of the spirit."

What I learned from our Creator is that if we ask for guidance he says, "I will answer you and I will show you great things and hidden things." When I did ask him for guidance, my first guidance was through my dreams and then through meditation. The word "logo" was coming to my mind. I needed to look for logos that had double meanings because this is how the Torah, the Bible, and the Quran are. We have to pay attention to all the books for God's true messages.

What others think, including in the Quran, is that if we pay attention to the life of Muhammad and everything he did and why and what he said, he also talks about unification. He recommended to all the ones who followed him to seek the truth in all the prophets, those including Jesus, Moses, and Abraham.

To be honest, in conclusion of all this research, meditation, and dreams, I see that Muhammad was a man who went through a lot of hardships since he was a child. There was a moment in his life that he needed God and God was there for him, just like with anyone else who needs Him. Everybody has been searching in the Bible, where Muhammad is in it in order to believe his message because everybody wants to see it through the scriptures literally word for word. If they understand that nothing in this earth moves without the will of God, they will understand that everything that is in this world, including Muhammad, is with the will of God, just like many people talk about the leaf falling from the tree at the precise moment, when God allows it to happen. No, in the Bible it does not say it in those specific words, but it explains that God is in control of every single thing on Earth and in Heaven.

If I can tell you one thing, Muhammad was a man in need, and when you have the need of God, he is always there for you as stated in the Bible. If you want to find a clearer form of what I am saying, I can tell you that Jesus, before dying, says this:

John 14:15 "If you love me, keep my commands. 16 And I will ask the Father, and he will give you another advocate to help you and be with you forever— 17 the Spirit of truth."

What I understand about Muhammad is that he is actually backing up Jesus and everything he said in the Bible. If you want to learn the truth, you have to stick to who was giving the messages. In this case, Muhammad was one of them who had the Spirit of Truth and is actually telling you to listen to Jesus, not to the spectators because everyone has their own opinion until today. It has nothing to do with the truth. We cannot judge the religions or people. Instead, we need to get to know them and understand them. If you want to know more about Muhammad, my suggestion is for you to read the Quran and you will know he will guide you through Jesus, with nothing but the truth.

Once you are with Jesus and you read the Bible, you have to follow his steps, just like he said, but don't get lost in the steps of the spectators. Just concentrate on what Jesus says and you will find the truth from his own words. After that, read about Moses because that is when God gave his name for the first time, I am that I am" and you will know why Jesus said "I am that I am." After that, read about Abraham and you will know that in the times of Abraham, God did not have a name. Many times Jesus stated in the Bible that he was not God. This is one of the examples:

Someone asked him "Lord, are only a few people going to be saved?" He didn't like the fact that this person was calling him "Lord."

That is why his answer was "Make every effort to enter through the narrow door, because many, I tell you, will try to enter and will not be able to. 25 Once the owner of the house gets up and closes the door, you will stand outside knocking and pleading, 'Sir, open the door for us.' "But he will answer, 'I don't know you or where you come from.' 26 "Then you will say, 'We ate and drank with you, and you taught in our streets.' 27 "But he will reply, 'I don't know you or where you come from. Away from me, all you evildoers!'"

Why did he talk about the narrow door and the big door? He did it because everybody is looking at the big door, which implies that he is the Lord. But if you listen carefully through his words, he was not lying. He requested in Matthew 7: 21-23 this: 21 "Not everyone who says to me, 'Lord, Lord,' will enter the kingdom of heaven, but the one who does the will of my Father who is in heaven. 22 On that day many will say to me, 'Lord, Lord, did we not prophesy in your name, and cast out demons in your name, and do many mighty works in your name?' 23 And then will I declare to them, 'I never knew you; depart from me, you workers of lawlessness.'

Why do you think he was so upset that he referred as "workers of lawlessness" to the people who called him Lord, cast out demons, and did mighty works in the name of Jesus? They are saying, "Lord, Lord did we not prophesy in your name..." as though meaning "we listened to you when you asked us to ask in your Father's name and not in your name." In reality, everything we were doing was prophesizing in the name of Jesus and not in the name of his Father, who is the true Lord.

In Matthew 24 he says 35 "Heaven and earth will pass away, but my words will never pass away. 36 But concerning that day and hour no one knows, not even the angels of heaven, nor the Son,[a] but the Father only."

I ask you why, if Jesus was God, he would not know when the last day is and strongly suggest to ask through his Father's will. And he said himself that he did not know and nobody but his father knows and he suggests for us to see beyond what everyone else sees, the big door.

Everyone is trying to get into Heaven by entering through the big door, which is outside of you. The narrow door is within you. He talks about Heaven and Earth passing away, but that his word will never pass away because now we are seeing the words he said and they have not passed away. And now through his own word we know he was not God, the Creator. And he doesn't know when the day will be that his Father will come. Why is that? We all know the definition of time. We all know that time is an illusion and that we all have different timings. Therefore, it cannot come at one time specifically for us because there is no time.

The Judgment Day is really being judged by others and condemned by others until you feel like having that conversation with God within you. The narrow door, in the Bible, is entering to the knowledge from what Jesus said, which is only the red part of the Bible, Moses, and Abraham. In the Torah, that narrow door to enter into the knowledge of truth is to learn about what Moses and Abraham said. In the Quran, the narrow door is what Prophet Muhammad, Jesus, Moses, and Abraham said. All of them, with no exceptions, were referring to our Creator and Provider of all because anyone can abandon you, but not our Creator.

When Jesus was crucified, it was the only time that Jesus doubted and was in fear. Being in doubt and in fear, according to the Bible, is dying. According to the Bible, the meaning of dying is sleeping. Our logical thinking is that dying is not being alive when according to the Bible dying is being alive. This is what is mentioned in Matthew 27:46

"46 About three in the afternoon Jesus cried out in a loud voice, "Eli, Eli,[a] lemasabachthani?" (which means "My God, my God, why have you forsaken me?").

That was to teach us that whenever we doubt, we live in condemnation. When we are in condemnation we are actually not alive because the Spirit of Life, which is the Spirit of God, is not there giving us life. When we are not in the Spirit of God, we are not alive. It is when we are sad, when we are condemned, when we are jealous, when we are judgmental or resentful. That is when not only are we dead, but we are in Hell. If we die, according to what death's definition is for us, with guilt, we die with that state of mind. Until, we realize time doesn't exist and that dying is being alive. And that is why we have Jesus explaining to one of his followers in Matthew 8:22 "But Jesus said unto him, Follow me; and let the dead bury their dead." When Jesus said this, Jesus could have said "let's meet somewhere else another day after you bury your father." Or "I will wait for you." But he wanted to make sure that we know dying doesn't mean what it is for us in our logical thinking. He was not being rude or sarcastic; neither when they let him know about Lazaro being dead for four days. Lazaro was not important, the importance was in the message, which is: What we think is dying is just sleeping. When Lazaro woke up, he did not know how long he had been asleep for or if he was dead or sleeping. In reality, when we go to sleep, we don't know how long we are asleep until we see the time.

THIS IS HOW JESUS EXPLAINED HOW WE ARE ONE AND HOW HE SAID HE WILL ASK HIS FATHER TO GIVE YOU ANOTHER SUPPORTER OF TRUTH

John 14:15 "If you love me, keep my commands. 16 And I will ask the Father, and he will give you another advocate to help you and be with you forever— 17 the Spirit of truth. The world cannot accept him, because it neither sees him nor knows him. But you know him, for he lives with you and will be[c] in you. 18(I will not leave you as orphans; I will come to you. 19 Before long, the world will not see me anymore, but you will see me in) . Because I live, you also will live. 20 On that day you will realize that I am in my Father, and you are in me, and I am in you. 21 Whoever has my commands and keeps them is the one who loves me. The one who loves me will be loved by my Father, and I too will love them and show myself to them."

And this is the true meaning of the book Unify.

MORE WAYS FOUND OF HOW WE ARE ONE IN THE BIBLE

Other Translations of Matthew 25:37
"Then shal the righteous answere him, saying, Lord, when saw we thee an hungred, and fedde thee? or thirstie, and gaue thee drinke?"
- King James Version (1611)

"Then the righteous will answer Him, 'Lord, when did we see You hungry, and feed You, or thirsty, and give You {something} to drink?'"
- New American Standard Version (1995)

"Then shall the righteous answer him, saying, Lord, when saw we thee hungry, and fed thee? or athirst, and gave thee drink?"
- American Standard Version (1901)

"Then will the upright make answer to him, saying, Lord, when did we see you in need of food, and give it to you? or in need of drink, and give it to you?"
- Basic English Bible

"Then shall the righteous answer him saying, Lord, when saw we thee hungering, and nourished thee; or thirsting, and gave thee to drink?"
- Darby Bible

"then will the righteous answer him, saying, Lord, when saw we thee hungry, and fed thee? or thirsty, and gave thee drink?"
- Webster's Bible

"`When, Lord,' the righteous will reply, `did we see Thee hungry, and feed Thee; or thirsty, and give Thee drink?"
- Weymouth Bible

"Then the righteous will answer him, saying, 'Lord, when did we see you hungry, and feed you; or thirsty, and give you a drink?"
- World English Bible

"Thanne iust men schulen answere to hym, and seie, Lord, whanne siyen we thee hungry, and we fedden thee; thristi, and we yauen to thee drynk?"

- Wycliffe Bible

"Then shall the righteous answer him, saying, Lord, when did we see thee hungering, and we nourished? or thirsting, and we gave to drink?"
- Youngs Literal Bible

Matthew 25:35-40
New International Version (NIV)
35 "For I was hungry and you gave me something to eat, I was thirsty and you gave me something to drink, I was a stranger and you invited me in, 36 I needed clothes and you clothed me, I was sick and you looked after me, I was in prison and you came to visit me.'"

This is how God is telling us he is in all of us, indiscriminately in all of us. Therefore, be careful when judging people because the other who you are judging is your reflection and God is in the other as he is in you.

I believe God is so disgusted in regards to people talking about each other or judging each other. This is what is in the Quran about judging others: It is like when you eat the flesh of your dead brother.

"We have discussed about backbiting. Now an

explanation of the Holy verse and its application to what we talked about. This Arabic word 'gheebat' (backbiting) should be pronounced with vowel 'ee' after the first letter 'g'. If it is read with vowel 'a' after 'g' it becomes 'ghaebat' meaning 'disappearance "…nor let some of you back bite others" (49:12)

This is a negative command. None of you should backbite some of you. This style of ordering is for stimulation, meaning you are one. O Muslims! Do not back bite your own selves.

مَيْتًا؟) أخِيهِ لحْمَ يَأْكُلَ أنْ أحَدُكُمْ (أيُحِبُ

"Does one of you like to eat the flesh of his dead brother? (49:12)"

THE LAST COMMAND FROM GOD THAT JESUS SAID

John 13:34
New International Version
"A new command I give you: Love one another. As I have loved you, so you must love one another."

My question to you is: are you on the side of God because God is one, he is unity and diversity, or are you on the other, the side of the others who want to destroy and separate? Which side are you on… one or another… just to be right. I realize it doesn't matter to be wrong some times as long as we find the truth... because our EGO is the one who cares about being right even when we know we may be wrong. But in my case I did not care about being wrong, I just wanted the truth for my soul, not for my EGO.

Now I understand when I'm reading what Jesus said, which I believe is true, but I learned to separate what is real and what is speculation.. I repeat that it is easier for a camel to go through the eye of a needle than for a rich man to enter the kingdom of God. Why are we talking about the Kingdom of God here on earth? And why do we need to put God above all things? The Kingdom of God is the spirit of life that gives us joy, peace, and power without much effort. The spirit of Our Creator cannot be purchased, not even with all the gold of the entire world. The Kingdom of God is not like you are going to Heaven in another place that is separate from Earth. The Kingdom of God starts here, living the Kingdom of God on earth, living free of difficulties, or at least learning to take them in a different, easier way.

When we say we are going to heaven, we are talking about a place in our mind, just like when we say we are going to hell, is as well, a place in our mind. That is why we sometimes see people complaining about life so much that they say this is not life, that this is hell. Sometimes they have made their lives so difficult for themselves in such a way that they fell that hell cannot be worse than what they already have. They get to a point in their mind that they want to get to hell and see if it is worse than what they are already going through. In the Quran, it states that Hell is underneath the first sky. In other words, hell or heaven is on earth. When I personally learned this, I started to feel more responsibility for myself and I understood more about free will. Now I know I cannot blame anybody else but myself for my outcome. Yes, there is hell, it is stated in the Bible, the Quran, and the Torah, but we misunderstood. They are talking about putting ourselves in that place of fire through our minds because that is the only way that we kill our spirit. We put our own spirit in hell.

I want to share this link with the readers of Unify. In this link, Andy Weir wrote a short story, in his own way, about how we are one. In Unify, I have different explanations of how this can be very possible, because we are one spirit of God living multiple lives.

www.galactanet.com/oneoff/theegg_mod.html

12 TIME AND MONEY

At this stage, in which I meditated in regards to time and money, was very intense. Although it is difficult to understand, and I still am having trouble understanding it, I have to talk about it. In the holy books it is talked about that the men back in those times lived many years –even up to 700 and 900 years.

Why do people now live so little time compared to these persons? For example, Adam and Abraham, according to the books, lived approximately 900 and 700 years. Now, the maximum is 70 to 120 years, according to the Bible. In the Guinness, in regards to longevity and according to its own investigations, it has been verified that Tomoje Tanabe of 113 years has lived the longest. They do not recognize Habib Mian who, due to his verifiable records, says he is 130 instead of 138 as the man who is and will continue being the oldest man in the world. At least the Guinness Book of Records recognized Mian Habib as the oldest man in the world in its 2005 edition.

That night I slept with more questions than answers. The curious thing was that as I fell asleep with that shower of doubts, it was like reviving and having all the questions I had while I was awake. However, this time, as I meditated through the night, I was obtaining the answers I needed. It was something inexplicable, but I was fascinated with it and would continue writing my book when I awoke. The answers in my dreams were so clear that the next day I could remember them very clearly.

This night was unique; it was an all-night meditation. By the end I didn't know if I was asleep or awake, but I finally awakened and continued thinking about this topic when I heard the voice. It told me, "You are tired. Sleep and tomorrow you will write what you dreamt and meditated." I turned halfway onto my bed to sleep. It felt like a lot for me, but in reality it had been short, maybe just minutes when the voice thundered in me. "Get up, it is time to write."

I said, "But I just fell asleep, how do you

expect me to wake up when I fell asleep only a few minutes ago?" It responded something; it was giving me a new idea for my deductions. He told me that we had condensed time in comparison to those ages when people didn't worry about time or money because to them it was an illusion, nothing more. He then asked me, "How long do you think you slept?" I thought it had only been an instant when he asked me to sleep until I awoke. I responded, "I don't know. Five to ten minutes, maximum." And the voice in my mind said, "But do you feel tired or well rested?" I said, "Well, I feel well rested, as if though I had slept all night."

His response was that this is how we had shortened time, by counting it in minutes. We did this because of a wish we had to live for a long time. We think we have the power to control it, but we don't. The power lies with our Creator. That is why we have shortened our time down to only minutes in life. Is that clear? There are some who only live and die within a matter of minutes. He continued to explain how time and money were an illusion and nothing more.

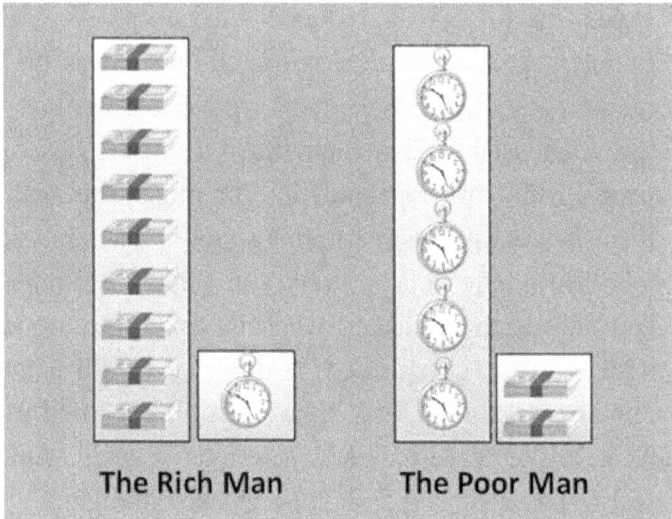

The Rich Man   The Poor Man

In the case of the rich: He wants to stretch time out because he has appointments and wishes to divide his time for the people he wishes to see. Otherwise, he would not even have time for him to enjoy his wealth. Even though money is not a worry for him as it was before, time is and the idea of not having enough of it.

On the other hand, the poor man has enough time, but that is not what he worries about. He worries about money because it generally does not make its way to his hands as he would like it to. He regularly has time to put food on the table and enjoy it with his family, something the rich man does not. However, the poor man does not have enough money and is always trying to stretch it out to cover all his expenses, essential or basic as they may be.

However, what counts is that they enjoy their passage on this earth. The poor are rich in time and the rich are rich in money, (what a great controversy) but at the end of it all, they are both ephemeral. You can't take either of those with you in the end. The rich try to stretch time in order to have more money, but they don't know they are simply administrators of what they think they have. Even so, they are still trying to make time to enjoy the money they have because at the end of the day they don't have time for themselves or to celebrate even holidays with their families. At the end of the day the only thing real in life is living from moment to moment.

Now, let's analyze the situation of the poor man. He is always busy looking for a way to obtain money in order to be happy and enjoy life (money buys only material, not happiness.) He does not realize that when he does obtain the money he only wants more because he thinks the more he has the happier he'll be.

In one of my dreams, he told me that on the other side of life, just like here; he is in control of time. It is intangible, so much so that when we die, he said it was like dreaming. It was a very profound dream that even if they tried to move us or do anything to our body, we could no longer wake up in this life. Dying is not like we think it is, when we die we confide our lives to an eternal dream. I would like to think that the dream we have when we die will be a continuation of where we left off in our expired life. It could be that we will pass on to a new life immediately. However, we may not be able to distinguish what exactly happens when we fall asleep and dream. Strange as our dreams may be, we never really know if we are dreaming or if we are awake. I have been confirmed in the Bible and in the Quran that dying is sleeping.

I believe I have already experienced this. I remember when I was a girl, about eight years old; I climbed a tree to cut a fruit. In one moment of carelessness, I fell from the very tall tree. When I touched the ground, I was unconscious and my mother's friend, who had accompanied me, picked me up immediately to take me to her. She cried desperately as she screamed for me to wake up. I felt myself telling her I was fine, and then yelling it, but neither she nor my mother could hear me because it was my internal voice. It was like a dream, it felt real, but it was not real for them as they held my unconscious body. Finally, I truly woke up and I explained to them that I was yelling at them that I was fine, but both said they had not heard me. They had felt for my pulse, but it was not there. However, I felt like I was still alive and had continued talking to them, but with no results. To their surprise, when I woke up, I described their efforts to wake me. I don't know if that was a case similar to the one when we truly die because I could talk without being heard. Perhaps it is just a short phase of the transition. I don't have any other explanation of that, even for myself.

Conquer Your Fears

I was meditating in regards to conquering fears. I thought, "What can kill God?" The answer was "nothing." In reality we fear about almost anything, but sometimes I think we enjoy fear without realizing it. Well, at least I think that fear allows us to know what we don't want. It is like clarification in our mind. We watch the news or videos online that give us the virus of the mind (fear.)

I believe now that I know the real name of God; I know that with him, everything is possible, and is within you. I wanted to share this because as I have learned to see things in a different way, I want everybody, as many as possible, to know this as well. When we are seeing everything in a negative way, without realizing it, we are acting with fear. Learning the meaning of fear helped me realize that it is just a thought in your mind that can be changed in a moment. I was not able to credit someone for this original idea, but this is the meaning of fear:

F alse
E vidence/Expectations
A ppearing
R eal

In reality, nothing can harm us unless we allow it to. We hear about air pollution, water contamination, vegetables with pesticides, meats with hormones, and medicine side effects that hurt more than they cure.

On the other hand, we have people who are eating car parts, broken glass, swords, swimming in extremely cold temperatures, and walking on fire. According to some, fire burns. Let's put it this way, if you ask one of the spectators that are watching people walk on fire, "why don't you try it?" his response will be "No way!" Why is that? If all those things are so bad for our health, then why do some people, knowing that the cigarette gives cancer, are still smoking while others die without having smoked at all?

"Your beliefs become your thoughts,

Your thoughts become your words,

Your words become your actions,

Your actions become your habits,

Your habits become your values,

Your values become your destiny."

-Gandhi

Why did God leave us the commandments and what is the first? Why do we lie? What is the necessity of lying? Why don't we trust him? It is because we feel we need to protect ourselves and not find ourselves in trouble and that we can solve it. We feel that if we tell the truth, we will have bad times and we think only we know it and no one will find out. But we forget that if we know it, He knows it, too. We forget that if we hear, he does as well. If we see, he does, too. If we think, so does him. In other words, he is inside us and he sees through our eyes and he can talk for us, without our authorization. He does not need permission to do all that. Why do we steal? Is it because we don't trust? What is the intention of stealing? It is because we do not trust him.

We feel that if we don't steal, we will not meet our needs, the ones we create at the moment we commit these offenses. Is there an excuse to steal? In other words, is there an excuse to believe God will not provide what we need?

Does he not have the capacity to do so? In other words, all the things we say to excuse ourselves from the faults we commit are nothing more than excuses for the lack of faith or trust in God. There are no white lies; those were created to protect our desires and guilt. Why do we kill? Because we feel we need to take vengeance into our own hands. For a moment we do not believe in divine justice. We want to solve everything in our own ways.

Why do we fornicate? Because we think there is more than what we have. Because we are always unsatisfied with what God has provided and we think we can hide from God. We can hide it from people and no one will know, but we forget that the one who can see is more important. We think that happiness is found in people, things, or money. The more we have, the more we want. We are never thankful or appreciate the moment. We always want to think ahead to the future because we think it will bring more of what we already have.

When I was meditating, I realized that science clings to a circle of reasoning without leaving its circumference. In regards to life, from the first day we were born, science tries to make us believe that we come from monkeys, that through evolution we became what we are now. My question is: then who made the monkeys? Who created the bang with which they claim earth was formed? If that is how it happened, can they create a similar explosion and create other humans in other worlds?

How can they prove what they speak about? For example, the question many of us ask ourselves, but no one has answered because they always base themselves on scientific experiments, is what came first, the chicken or the egg? Those who believe in God know that our Creator created all animals in couples and even science knows we are rational. My question is, why they don't realize once and for all that the chicken came first along with the rooster, made by our Creator and then told to reproduce.

Scientists have continually asked that question to confuse people, but they have not realized they are the confused ones. With such a silly question, they will never find an answer. If they took the time and focused on those who have been cured of diseases deemed "terminal" by science, would they know the cause of them being cured? A profound investigation was conducted (by experts on the matter in question) and at the end it was found they were cured by faith, because those who have their hopes in the abilities of the doctors die waiting for a remedy for their illness.

With this in mind, I'm not saying that no doctors believe in God. In fact, I'm sure there are and those who do pray for their patients are more successful than those who don't believe they need God. To the doctors who don't believe they need God, the ones who think they are superior, I give them a challenge: to sculpt a man of clay or mud. If they are good sculptors they may be able to form a very good human body, perhaps even a perfect replica. However, can they give it life? That is my question.

Another controversial topic is abortion. In regards to this, I ask you what your stand on it is. Do you think we have the right to end a life? In my opinion, I think not. Do not let doctors, confuse you. Meditate for a second if you are contemplating abortion as a solution. What does our Creator think of what I am about to do? How does he view this? He is the only one who can give life. I know the "doctors" tell you, especially if it is an early stage in pregnancy that the fetus has not yet formed, that it is only a period that has accumulated and, therefore, there is nothing wrong with what you are doing.

They tell you that it's only your period being late a couple days because that's what they want you to believe. Don't listen to them, it's something they do for money, it's their business. Out of experience, I tell you this: what you are ending is something our Creator has planned. It's a beautiful gift and you will never know what it would have been like. This gift of life is a privilege not given to everyone in the world (some people will never be given this privilege.) That human being will be your reason to live. When I see my own children I understand that it is the biggest gift I have been given. Would you have liked it if your own mother had done that to you, taken your chance of knowing what life is? Is it not perturbing to think of that?

During my meditation I had the opportunity to ask our Creator in regards to the cloning and if he was allowing it. His response was the same that he is the one who gives life and cloning an organism is only cloning the shape of the body he has already created. After all, "the body is just a disguise" and that disguise can only be given life by him. In other words, it's like grafting two trees. We are not giving life; we are just changing the design of the body. We are copying it and pasting it, but not giving it the soul and spirit of life. After some thinking, I wondered if that baby they cloned would like to be the way they made him. They would not be asking for his opinion. In fact, they may ruin his life because it would have been without his authorization and he will always wonder how his life would be if they didn't copy him from another.

The point here is that we as human beings get confused because we know God is with us and in us thinking that we are God and we can create anything we want, but when we think we are God, we are separating ourselves from God. It is our ego trying to show we can do better. When that happens that it is when we fail in our creation. God is our Provider in every single thing we have and do.

SONIA AHMED

13 MY MOTHER'S JOURNEY

I had the opportunity of spending my mother's last days in the hospital with her, talking with her. She was 75 years old and had been profoundly religious during her lifetime. Although we didn't practice the same religion, we united by faith in her last days. Due to the advancement of her illness, I knew time was limited. I had this opportunity to talk with her and I knew I needed to make the most of it. I had many unanswered questions and I knew this was the moment to ask her about them before she abandoned her body. In regards to my doubts and questions, they were all answered. The lovely thing about it all was that she was completely conscious the whole time up to the last breath in her body. I remember one of my questions was "Mother, what you think of the religion I practice?" I had asked her the same question before and her response had been to ask me another question. She had asked if after changing religion my God continued being the one who created Adam and Eve. My response had been "yes, it is him." However, I decided to ask her once more before I let her go.

"Mother, what do you think of the religion I practice?" I asked her again.

She replied, "God is love, not religion. It does not matter what religion you belong to or follow. You could do everything that is asked of you, but if you are not connected to God by faith, it makes no sense. The important thing is to be connected with him by faith every single day of your life because if you have faith, you don't need to see something to believe it. When you are connected to God there is no fear, hate, grudges, envy, or vanity. God is all the opposite, it's true, he is truth, love, compassion, understanding, humbleness, and generosity."

After she explained this to me, there came a moment when she felt sleepy and she described the feeling like one when someone is very tired and hasn't slept in many hours. It was the kind of exhaustion that overpowered someone's will to stay awake; its strength is greater than your own. Finally, you give in letting yourself live that last moment left in that unique, perfect costume that was designed just for your soul.

Wherever you are at the moment, stop and look at how we are all unique (one.) We are all one to God, without repetition, without being the same. From the place where you stand take a look at your surroundings and see the faces of the people who are there and you will not find one face the same as another. As much as you try, even in twins, you will always find a difference. Getting back on topic in regards to my mother, something that happened on her last day was that she ate one last time before she passed away. She no longer felt hunger, but I begged her to do it and, since I so insisted, she finally accepted.

However, she told me, "Alright, I will eat, but I have asked God that the sustenance my body is obtaining does not reach me. I ask that it reaches all those bodies of the ones who do not have food to eat because of illness or scarcity."

We then took each other's hands and prayed to God for all the people who were in need of him, in faith, so that he may enter them and guide them. Later, she alone began to pray to God for me so he could give me wisdom to guide my family and those who surrounded me and she said that was her last wish. During that moment when her soul still resided in her body, before abandoning it, she told me she felt a pain in her soul. It was something that, among other types of pains, I had never heard of, but I asked her, "Mother, what is that pain like?" And she told me it was an unexplainable pain like she had never felt before.

Now sitting beside the lifeless body of my mother, I realized that no matter how much I tried speaking to her, it was no more than the "costume" she had used in this visible world. Also, that her soul was no longer in her body and that dying is like when someone is falling asleep, but not knowing once they've fallen asleep. Ask yourself how you feel when you are sleepy, tired, exhausted with no will to stay awake, all those feelings you feel before falling asleep. You ask yourself, "Am I asleep?" and you answer yourself that you are not. But when you are asleep you no longer feel, you are not conscious, you can't see, and if you do, you go through situations in your dreams. You don't have control of what happens or stops happening because you are letting your subconscious take over, but at the same time absolutely everything is real no matter how silly or incredible your dream is. You don't even know it isn't real until you wake up from it and realize it was just a dream and nothing of what you experienced was of what we call until now "real life" because we have not experimented anything else and that is all that is in our mind. Stop for a moment and ask yourself, what of all this is real after all?

When a rich person dies, or any other person, people ask, "How much money did he leave?" And the answer is: everything. He left everything; the amount is irrelevant because in the end he will not take anything, not even the body he thought he owned. I think based on what I have read, and the form in which I can perceive everything, that this is the phase we call life. God created everything in abundance and when people say that there is no food, it is not true. There is food in all the stores; they throw away food, fruit, vegetables, and meat every day. The truth that I have been able to observe is that we have distributed it wrongly. If the owners of those stores were more conscious and thought of not wasting it, they could store it a day before throwing it out, before it went to waste, and send it to places where it could be useful. But no, we do not want to do that because we are always thinking of our convenience, of the way by which only we can be benefited because if there is no personal benefit then there is no reason for it to be.

They shall start creating excuses, for example, "if we do this, people will get sick because of the food we have sent and they will sue us." Or simply the fact that they have enough to eat daily will make it seem like an extra, unnecessary cost, with no monetary benefit to the company because the benefit they expect is artificial.

Something that comes to my mind when I touch this topic is that I grew up in a home of abundance, thanks to God. My mother had a store and in my house there were always fruits and vegetables. We had plenty to eat at any given moment and she practiced what I now speak of. She never threw food away because she always distributed it at its moment. One day, when I was sitting at the table, eating, a neighbor's daughter came and when she saw the appetizing fruits on the table, she asked my mother for one. And she, without thinking twice, asked her to pick the one she wanted and the girl did. At the time I was also a girl and I watched her with jealousy in my eyes. Although I did not say anything to either of them, my mother could observe my look and what I was thinking and she asked me, "In what place would you rather be, in a place of abundance where you have enough to give away or in a place of poverty where you have nothing and need to ask for it?"

I didn't answer because I had nothing to say. I just sat there analyzing and she continued speaking about how important the act of being thankful was, about being on the side of abundance and sharing because nothing of what we have is ours. As much as we wanted to be the owners of it, in her way of explaining, she told me that a tortilla, in order to cook properly, had to be flipped. She was telling me that in other words, the coin has two faces and to better understand the meaning, we have to understand the person in the other situation, contrary to the one we are in. If we don't achieve understanding, God will put us at that level to experiment what that person is feeling at that moment in their life. It is just a phase, just a moment, and what she wanted to avoid was me thinking that if I shared I would run out.

Just the simple act of thinking in scarcity was as if though I had began to plant a seed in my mind that I could not share because what I had in front of me was mine and if I shared it, it would be gone.

Children don't know much of what it is to share or about practically anything in general of what life is. As mothers, we want to help many times by telling them they need to share their new toy or the bag of fruit we have picked for them if we are at a park and a child wants some. However, as humans, we often forget that we tend to learn what we see as children rather than what we hear. We want them to understand with explanations that something is good, but we forget that, as adults, they copy or imitate what they see in us, not what we say. They learn through example and often times they end up being selfish like us parents. We teach them not to believe in abundance because there is only enough for them, that there is a limit and not to share. At the end of it all, it is a consequence of the way we perceive things.

I suppose in her mind she thought "I have this much, enough to give away and share" and not "I have this much, enough to throw away without caring if others don't have any. That's their problem, not mine." Many of us see it that way and think in that form because we think we are the ones who have worked for that, but we don't recognize it is God who has provided for us. We think it is because of work that we have made or achieved, but we don't recognize that he has also provided our job until we have nothing. It is then that we understand God is the one who has provided for us as with everything else. It is when we search and ask of him when he provides and only then will we understand that all we have is not because of us, but because of him.

On the other hand, when you don't understand what you are living or experiencing in your life, it will be greater and more difficult because you don't know what is the reason for what you are going through. It is necessary to finally understand in order to grow spiritually.

That is why we see cases in which some people get lost, because they don't understand the message. In some cases, as the situation gets more difficult, people even lose their minds because they can't find themselves. If you stop to think about it, we all know what we do and don't want. However, we tend to emphasize what we don't want and spend more time thinking of what we don't want than on what we do want from this life. Just think, there is enough water for everyone if we look for it. There is so much that the world is surrounded by it. There is also a lot of money in the world and if you stop to think of the whole world, there is no one who could say with exactitude how much there is. If someone tried to count it, there would be more by the time they finished because more is produced daily all over the world.

I think that God, like it says in all his holy books, has created everything in abundance for those of us who are with him on earth. What makes us think otherwise? It is our enemy that acts in our mind to lead us astray, saying things like "steal, no one's looking or you'll be left with nothing," "Lie; after all, you're the only one who saw. Nobody will know anything," "Take justice into your own hands and you'll be fine."

However, you don't know that revenge poisons your soul and kills. Don't fear the one who kills the body, but the one who kills the soul. What he doesn't want is attachment to things because when we do that, we grow dependent of it. There is a point when we even convert it into our God, like money and material things and there are many times when people do it.

It is a marvelous experience seeing the beginning and end of life in front of me, how it forms and covers the soul and then when the soul abandons the body as it leaves.

Experiencing the act of being here, I understood why God doesn't want us to become attached to anything, not even our body. It is because thinking that way is the way we can have everything and enjoy every minute. It is just an experience of having it and then leaving it without difficulty, like all things because when we consider ourselves the owners of everything (like money) we begin to exert vanity, pride and begin to see others as less than what we are. We begin to think we are superior because we think we have obtained all this by our own means and that they belong to us. And in order to defend that idea, we even kill for it. The same happens with people, things, or even worse, our body. Yes, it is the home occupied by our soul, but it is just a home, a suit molded uniquely for our soul.

Many times we ask ourselves why so many things that make us suffer in one way or another happen. Then we ask God to help us and we feel he does not listen to us, but he does to others. Then we ask the ones he does listen to for help so that God may hear us also, but even through them, God will not hear what we ask of him.

After all this, I have realized that the reason why we think he has not given us what we ask for is that we indirectly refuse to receive what we are asking for when we turn it away with any doubts we have. If we have faith, we don't need someone to intervene for us. Faith was not made for someone special, for some and not for others; it was made for everyone just like with everything God created. However, the way we perceive it is the way to obtain it. There is a saying that every head is a world and if we analyze it a bit, in a certain way every mind is a world created by each person, by individual logic. It is that simple, "every person ends up living what they end up believing." It is just what you choose to project. It has been very clear that all that happens is not bad, they are situations we need to live in order to grow and go on to the next level. The situations we live are no more than contrast to what we need to go through in order to choose what we really do and don't want to experience in our lives

14 ANALYZING MORE THAN WE CAN SEE

Recently, I went on a trip with my children, a six year old and the other of 13, to Las Vegas, Nevada. My older son decided he wanted to go see the exhibition at the hotel Luxor, one of human bodies. At that moment I didn't know if it would be a good idea to take him because I thought maybe he would get scared at the idea of seeing lifeless bodies. In other times it would have probably even scared me.

My son said, "Please, Mom. I want to go see it."

The exhibition had human bodies from skeletons to other bodies. It was interesting to look at them, all those lifeless, dried bodies. However, nothing impacted me as much as seeing fetuses. They had real humans from six weeks, at which they are a small, round dot the color of bone, to a few weeks before the nine months of pregnancy. It was all in an exact sequence, showing how that small dot as it goes, growing longer through the weeks. It is seen growing longer, taking the shape of an egg, and then taking a round shape until it looks like a fish. Then, an incision forms in the lower part, forming legs. Slowly, it begins taking the complete shape of a baby. You might think, I already know this, I have seen it many times in magazines, books, videos, and I've even had my own baby, in a woman's case. However, the astonishing thing was seeing it up close, so real, unlike in books, magazines, or videos.

I thought about how in the Torah, the Bible, and the Quran, it is mentioned that we should fear the one who kills the soul, not the body. With the help of my six year old I could see the way his eyes perceived everything. It was incredible to appreciate everything before our eyes. I told him, "look that is what you were like before you became what you are now." What I showed him at that moment, when he was already visible, was meant to happen, I think. Now, I can truly describe what went on in my mind that day. It was then that I truly realized our body was just a disguise, uniquely made for our soul to make it visible to our eyes. When our soul arrives, it comes without a disguise, but it uses this one for its period of life and when it is over, it abandons it and leaves without it. Even the last day on earth needs to be visible for it to be credible. Interesting, isn't it?

15 SUPERSTITIONS

I asked our creator regarding superstitions. Are they real? Well, superstitions are simply thoughts passed on by our ancestors, like cooking recipes, that for one reason or another associated something with a situation someone was going through. For that same reason they felt it had influenced that moment even though perhaps it had just been a coincidence and they chose to blame it on that specific event. Perhaps it didn't have anything to do with what had occurred.

A superstition is a way of manipulating the mind in order to live in fear and not in faith. A few examples of superstitions is spilling salt, breaking a mirror, or walking under a ladder. We need to change those "recipes" if they make no sense or have no benefits. After all, it is only in your mind and our creator is the one who is in control of it all. Forget superstitions and let our Creator control your mind with thoughts that will make you feel good. Superstitions are an example of irresponsibility when something happens and we look for something to blame. Every thought has a root and so did all these superstitions, contagious and passed on until today. They were passed on by those who did not want to accept responsibility and therefore blamed the salt for spilling and other things that had nothing to do with what is now causing fear and unstable emotions. You don't need to believe what you are thinking, just remember that who is in control of everyone and everything is our Creator. Go to the park and observe the birds and plants; watch how they move and think about how it all happens without you doing anything to make it happen. Yet, it is all happening because our Creator is in control of everything and the moment you are in is about to change and all you have to do is enjoy the moment because the present will always be the present. And the present will be an infinite moment because, going back to time, time does not exist.

16 HOW TO ACTIVATE FAITH IN A LOGICAL FORM

I asked myself that question. It would be... Just trying to be illogical because faith is like a concentration of pure, positive energy there is nothing fake because you cannot pretend to feel something you don't feel because our creator knows when we are faking something. In a way, it is giving vitamin faith to hope. But if I can describe it, it would be just trying to be illogical. Allow yourself to be directed with thoughts and you have control over the steering wheel. Yes, that would be a way of thinking of it with logic. "If I have to believe in something that I cannot see, something I have asked of God with faith, like asking for health when I am ill and can't see God, have I been granted it? Everything that I am seeing is with the analysis the doctor is showing me and what he is telling me."

Pretend what he just said to you in that moment is just another diagnostic to what God had told you previously. That diagnostic in front of you is wrong, well it is about to change. And don't fear, just trust that it will come.

To continually stay in faith, I need to simulate I have been given a role in a movie, one in which I need to act. The role in the movie is that I am completely healthy and I am well. I enjoy perfect health and need to act like it every day and keep practicing it until I can play the role I was assigned so well that everyone else and I believe it until the end of the filming, ready to be released for viewing by everyone.

It could be that role or any in the movie that I have asked for to God. What happens if God doesn't want to give me said role? It is because he has another one, a better one for me, one that is unknown to me, but it is always better than what I am asking him to act. The role that he has designated for me will come in a better situation in life; it will probably be the role of a protagonist. That is considering an act of asking God in faith.

We should also never forget of the present, a

gift God gives each day, thanking him for it, considering the change that is about to arrive. Although it is not always visible, prepare to receive it: that beautiful present that has not arrived yet, but imagine being there with only your thoughts.

When you have contrary feelings to the ones you have asked for just say, "I am in faith and what I am thinking and seeing is just a moment about to change." Many times we think things that are not true. When that sensation of negativity returns, remember it is only a thought, nothing more. Also, keep in mind that you have the ability to change it to something more positive, something that will make you feel better than the sensation the other was causing you.

To be honest, of all the bad thoughts we have we are not with them 100% and by doing this continually you could change your way of feeling slowly, every day. For example, music: Listen to that which has good messages; it will help raise your mood just as much as meditating.

Eat healthy, exercising your body will help you change your mood and make you feel thankful for all that you have, starting with the ability of breathing and all else that you can perceive at that moment of your life.

When you make this call of conscious, there will go by a series of situations within you. Beforehand, I want you to know it is normal what you will think and feel, but they are necessary for you to find yourself first.

Many times we ask our Creator for something and he gives it to us at the moment, but there are other times when he tells us, "No, it is not the moment." I feel like in a way he is the music and we need to wait to sing at the right time because otherwise we will sound out of tune and awful. When we are out of tune with God, we are miserable and uncomfortable. When you are in tune, you are in peace, you are happy, you are positive, you are patient, and you are at ease –the opposite of disease. Depending on how you ask is how you will receive. There will be occasions where you think he is not answering you, but all that will be in your expectations. When you don't expect it to happen, ask our Creator: Why am I not expecting this to happen? Is it because I am seeing everything in a logical way and I am not seeing it in faith? If that is the case, allow me to see with your eyes what is about to come. Being honest is the best way in that one on one conversation because the Creator knows when you're not expecting things to happen.

About five years ago, my husband and I wanted to buy a property that we were able to afford cash. I was excited for it; it was a house by a lake and we would have used it as a vacation home. Since the home we wanted to buy was in Guatemala, I could not buy it myself and instead it would be bought in my sister's name. I asked God to allow me to buy that property if it would not give me problems or bad experiences, moneywise, or any other type of situations that I would not like to experience later on, knowing he knows more about me than myself and knowing he knows about my future more than myself. However, it did not happen. The transaction did not occur even though I could afford it. The man who was selling it refused to give the papers of the house and I refused to give him the money first. The lawyer involved told me he was not liable for anything if he did not have the papers and I decided I should not do it. I was confused because he complicated it because he knew it was something I would not like to experience. During my lifetime I have always asked God this way, to make it possible if there is something I would like to experience for any reason or if it is convenient to me. I learned to feel that it was something I should not do. Back then, I did not see anything wrong with the property; I could even imagine myself already at that house. A few months after this, my sister was killed and I realized if I had bought the property, I would have lost all the money I had used. There are things God does that we may not like, but he does it to keep us from having bad experiences. There is a saying that says there is no bad thing that comes without a good reason. Sometimes, we later on realize there are experiences we need to go through in order to go on to a different level of understanding and to see the things God wants or don't want for us. We may not always prepare because we don't know what is coming in the future, but God always knows.

Something that's true of all this is that I have learned he does not improvise. He always has a plan for everyone. We are the ones who do not know it; we go astray causing ourselves pain. He is simply challenging us to believe in his word because when he says no, it is because he has something better planned for us. It is a better plan than the one we have because we always think our plans are better than his.

We forget that trials we go through make us blind to reality and that is why we can't achieve to see our plans. He knows we can't and many times that we believe we can do whatever we want without paying consequences. Then, when people try to make us wake up by helping us see that there is a price to pay for all we do, we say, "Oh, I know that is the price and it is worth it because I am going to do what I want and finally be happy."

However, every single time the price is higher than what we were willing to pay because we always focus on how beautiful it could have been, what we want to see, like in a fairytale. Cinderella is a good example. What we don't realize is our Creator has made a specific pay for each of us, one we refer to as the final account, and yet we continue to act in a way that we hurt each other's.

Every time we think about doing something to someone, let's think it over and place ourselves in their shoes to see what it feels like. When the coin flips, will you be able to handle the price you will really pay?

I searched, out of my own curiosity, the meaning of "faith" in the dictionary and it gave me a series of responses, but they all share this in common: Depending on the religion, faith believes in God or Gods, in a doctrine, it is the form of teaching religion. Faith can be big and includes trust and believing without evidence in sight of everyone.

Faith is regularly substituted by hope, trust, or believing what some critics have discussed, that faith is the opposite of reasoning. It is that which cannot be negotiated with because of lack of evidence. This is like an example of what will happen with the future that by definition has not been seen, yet.

The definition in regards to who is God or what is God like:

God is light, but he is more than that. In Islam, it says that God has 99 names, like previously mentioned. He has many names, he is all that but in reality he is what he needs to be with you at the moment you need him. He is "I am." He is with everyone, with me like with you, like he is in the body of the homeless, indiscriminately. He is there regardless of your color or whether you are aware of him or not.

God is the divine light, but nobody can see him even though he can see in all of us, in our very own eyes. God is above all comprehension. Yet, he knows everything. In other words, we cannot understand him, but he understands us. We cannot see him, but he does see us. The only thing we have control over is belief. We need to believe even if we can't see his finished works and they are all a beautiful surprise in the end when we believe in him firmly even though to the others it will seem illogical or lacking in common sense all that is about to happen. Since in its moment it did not have common sense, many things didn't make sense before existing since their creators had not yet discovered them and they wouldn't have done it without the help of God.

That can only occur within our thoughts.

This morning I reached my office and I don't know for what reason, when I tried to turn my computer on it said "Out Of Range." I thought, is this how we feel when we don't have faith? We need and tell God, our Creator, "look how many debts I have and I don't have money to pay them. Only you know why you don't help me. God, you see my situation, why don't you help me?" For whatever reason we may be thinking of, we feel we are not connected. As much as we try, we don't feel the message we want to send is being received because we are completely disconnected.

The connection is there, it's available. It is us who need to find how to connect, but there are times we don't see it and that is what I am trying to show in this book. I am trying to use logic in everything, the most possible to achieve this purpose. After finishing the definition of what faith is, I realized our Creator has everything planned out. He does not improvise, the ones who never finish improvising is us. We make so many plans, "Plan A," "Plan B," even "Plan C" and many more. He only has one that he PRE-destined for us. It is what our subconscious talks to us about and we ignore it all the time. It is what we are missing out on, but when we finally discover it, plan B or C stops existing and our concentration will be Plan A, the master plan.

I want to give an example of this because I found the response while I tried to explain the book.

If our Creator planned that this month you will win an example quantity of $5,000.00, he has predestined this and has put the amount in your mind. You know said amount for some reason and it is the amount you need this month, why? It is because he planned it for you. Now, how will you make that money? He will put alternatives as a test to see if you will acquire it honestly. He puts option A. Will you do it in an honest way? Option B is there even though he has already predestined it for you and you will obtain it.

Obviously, at the end of it all, you want to follow Plan C because the ability has been given to you and the possibility of obtaining it. If he gave you this thought, he can also give you the ideas of how, where, and when it will happen. He will open doors or will close them if you think it was only your idea and you don't need God and you are self-efficient, that is your EGO. He will make it impossible if it is not within his plans.

All of this, he gives it to you in that feeling we all have, the one scientists call the sixth sense. It is the one that gives us reassurance of something or hesitation, ability or inability, peace or agony, but when we are confused, we don't know that to do nothing is the best thing. Also, we need to meditate in order to find the best answer to our internal voice.

That is what our reasoning is for and we need to be careful because when we justify, it is only our feeling of culpability. It is what our internal voice is talking about when we have done something wrong and it will not leave us alone until we accept it and stop hiding it.

17 DISTINGUISHING THE INTERNAL VOICE THAT SPEAKS TO US

When I was in this stage of the book, I asked myself this and later meditated over it. I asked our Creator to help me know how to distinguish if it was him, me, or even worse, when it was Satan who was talking to me at that moment or with any bad purpose or when it was simply me remembering a loved one that came to mind.

The answer came to me the same day. I was driving to the supermarket, but there was a stop in the route to let pedestrians cross. The people there looked at me as though asking, will you let us cross? A voice told me, let them cross. I listened to that voice and gestured with my hand so they would. When those people were in front of my car, another voice told me run them over with the car. At that moment the immediate answer within me was no, no… I am not crazy.

It was in that moment that that voice told me, *I know, that is why I said that to you at that moment. I know who you are and what you think, but I wanted to let you know when it was me and when it was not. I am generous, merciful; I was the one who told you to let them cross, but when you heard the voice to run them over, that was the voice of wrong. That is why I have given you reasoning, so you can listen to that voice and be able to distinguish between mine and the voice of bad and to make the correct decisions. There will be moments in everyone's lives when it will be difficult to distinguish between good and bad. The bad hides so well it can confuse you.*

Now I understood what the voice of good was and what my voice was. There are also other forms that help distinguish between the good and bad. It is in our feelings. For example, when you do something good for someone (you have probably tried this) you feel like a hero inside. When, on the contrary, you do something bad you feel culpability even if you don't say it. You feel it and many times you yourself uncover it while trying to cover it with lies. When you are in that lapse of confusion the best thing is to not do anything until you clear your mind.

It is the same thing with our sense of smell. It, too, can give us a form of feeling. For example, when you smell a fragrance and it brings you memories and your mind immediately takes you years back. Without a doubt, our mind is a wonderful machine; it is so powerful in the way that we find reason in everything. Many times it even makes us feel things we can't even see. If you don't believe me let me demonstrate it. Right now, imagine you have a lemon in your hand. Now, slice the lemon in two pieces. Take one half and squeeze it in your mouth, imagine it clearly. I assure you, if you concentrate, you will be able to feel the acidic taste of the lemon. You can try this with other fruits and I assure you could even pass the feeling on to someone else with your own mind.

Try it. That is why people say emotions are contagious, because they are pure energy. If you'd like to experiment, go ahead. If you want to make someone feel tired, whoever it is that is near you, just pretend you are sleepy and try to yawn in front of them. Keep doing it and you'll see that very soon that person will start yawning as well. You can also do it when you are crying. If you remember a sad moment in your life it will make you cry. Well, you can also make the person next to you cry. Also, if you want to make them laugh without telling a joke, just start laughing. Soon enough you'll see that person is laughing and they won't even know why.

There are times when we don't even need positive words to share the energy of the act. Just by watching you cleaning your house, whoever is there will also catch the energy.

On one occasion, our neighbor told us, my husband and I, that we passed our energy on to him because we were cleaning our garden so enthusiastically that he started cleaning his. That energy works with our reasoning, but we need to be conscious of what type of energy we want to attract that day and generate it in our thoughts with our reasoning.

Coming back to that internal voice, Jesus said that the spirit of God is the space in between the mind and the soul. I now believe there is no specific place to listen to our Creator; when you have the need and have the questions the spirit of our Creator knows. I truly believe that when you have that need he is just there waiting for you and there is no specific place for it, it just happens, it works in a way just like a phone call. Don't feel shy or scared when you hear that voice because at first it will sound strange, but it will be like it's yourself telling you things. That voice will come as an answer all of a sudden or a question to you and you will know it's not you because you were not thinking about that. Many people like to do it in a quiet place or room, but that voice can come to you at any given time; in a moment of silence.

18 MIRACLES

During my life, I always heard people talking about miracles that had happened to them or things they saw that they couldn't explain in a logical way. Somehow, all my life I was not religious or as close to God as I am learning to be now. To be honest I don't consider myself that religious, I am just trying to understand life through our Creator, since he is the maker of life. I was just an average person. Sometimes, when people used to tell me their stories about what happened to them, to be honest, I had a hard time believing them. I always thought they were making stories up. That is, until they started happening to me.

Miracle 1

That is when I remembered my mother. When I was about ten years old my mother was praying for a family friend that was a non-believer and had passed away. Those nights, my mother was sharing her bed with one of my aunts that had come over to the house for a week on vacation. My father was not at home so my aunt would sleep in the same bed, along with my mother. My mother was Catholic so, in the corner of her room, she placed a cup of water containing some fresh flowers from her garden, dedicated to the person who had passed away. One night, before going to bed, she was praying for that person in her room. Right after praying, she went to the bed, where my aunt was already sitting. As soon as she covered herself with the blanket, getting ready to sleep, the flowers came floating towards her of their own accord and just dropped on her. My mother and aunt were both surprised because it felt like it was a sign that her prayers had been accepted. They did not know how those flowers, on their own, had come towards them. That night, they both had a hard time going back to sleep because it was something that they could never explain in a logical world.

Miracle 2

When I was about nine years old, there was a

lady who was my mother's friend that had come over to the house for vacation. I used to live in a small town; the bathroom of that house was a bit far off from the main house, like the bathrooms in small villages, with no drainage; a septic tank bathroom.

On that day, we had lunch together with our friend in the house. Right after lunch, my mother's friend decided to take a nap with her two kids. The older one was about six years old and the younger one was three years old. I went to the room where they were having their nap with their mother. When I saw them sleeping, I decided to go out and play by myself in the garden because I was not tired.

It was boring because I did not have anyone else to play with. I decided to just sit down by myself under the tree. About five minutes after that, the three year old child came out of the room and walked to the bathroom by himself. I was surprised because even his older brother was scared to go on his own, the bathroom being approximately 400 feet away from the room they were sleeping in. When I saw him go in by himself, I decided to scare him. So, I hid behind a bush and stayed there about 15 minutes, waiting until he came out. However, the time went by and he was not coming back. I decided to go and check inside the bathroom because I saw him go in, closing the door of the bathroom. I had even heard the noise from the door closing, but he never came back out. There was no other way out but through that door in order to come back to the house. I went inside the bathroom to check on him because I thought maybe he had fallen inside the tank, but there was nobody there. I was amazed, wondering what had happened to him.

I ran back to the house to talk to his mother, but when I entered the room, I saw him sleeping in the same place he was before I had gone outside to play.

I asked the mother, "Where was your three year old son?"

"He has been sleeping for a while," She told me.

"No, but he went to the bathroom right now," I said.

She responded, "No, when he goes to the bathroom I go with him because he is scared to go on his own."

After she explained that to me, I started crying because I had seen him and my question was: If he was not the one, then who went to the bathroom that looked exactly like him? That question was never answered.

Miracle 3

My husband and I had just started our life together when I went from California to Las Vegas with him for the first time. We had a car with no air conditioning and we were driving during the summertime around 2 P.M. There were no clouds in the sky; it was blue everywhere at every angle we could see. It was my first time going there, so when I saw the Rocky Mountains on my left hand side, I asked my husband to pull over and go over towards them. It was so hot that the sting was coming up from the pavement. I did not have any water with me so I started feeling dehydrated with a headache.

I said out loud, "Oh my God, I wish it could rain."

My husband overheard me and with a laugh said, "Yeah, right."

When I heard that, in my mind, I thought God, I wish you could do this just to show him that it can happen. Two minutes after that, it started raining. When the water started falling on our car, my husband was astounded. He stopped the car and opened the door. He got out of the car to find where the water was coming from. To his surprise, there was one cloud right above our car, raining just for us. My husband went back inside the car and he said to me, "You should ask to win the Lotto." When he said that, I also got out of the car because I was amazed at what was happening. I also saw the cloud above the car. I went inside the car and my husband just turned the car off because we were off the road and waited approximately five minutes until there was no more water falling on our car. There was just one cloud to rain for us. To this day, it continues being a magical moment in my life.

Miracle 4

We need to pay attention to our dreams, knowing that not all the dreams are true, but some of our dreams can be a warning of something that may happen or already happened. The reason why I am saying this is because I experienced in my life many dreams that have become true like on this occasion:

There was a time that I was on vacation in the country I was born in. My husband had at that time decided to let me extend my vacation with my family for four more days. He decided to bring our two kids with him so I could enjoy the time with my family. When he came to California, he went to a party at the house of a friend that we have known for a long time. Something happened at that party that I did not know about and my husband did not want to tell me about. I don't know why.

The point is that when I came back from my vacation, my husband said to me, "Let's go and visit our other friends."

They were related to the friends that had held the party in their home in California. We spent the weekend with them, but at night, when we were sleeping in their house, I had a dream of exactly what had happened at that party, of what my husband had not wanted to tell me.

The next morning, after I woke up, I sat down with the other couple to have breakfast with them. While having breakfast, I recalled the dream I'd had the night before and I said to the wife, "You know, I had this weird dream last night that we were at a party and your brother in law attended it, not with his wife, but with someone else other than his wife. We were very surprised because we have been seeing him with his wife for about ten years and no one knew what was happening, not even the family. It was a surprise to us all."

When I told her that, she turned to my husband and asked, "Did you tell her what happened at the party?"

I was not aware of any party since I was not in the country when it was held. My husband was surprised and explained then that he had not told me anything. I was then confused because I did not know what was going on.

So, I asked her, "Why are you asking him that? What happened?"

My husband then explained to me that everything that happened in my dream was true, even the way I described the lady. I believe that when God wants you to know something he lets you know somehow, in some way.

Miracle 5

In my life, nothing out of the ordinary was happening until I started experiencing a lot of hardships in my life in such a way that I really got away from being close to God. It was so bad that I was kind of denying his existence until recently in December 2012, when I started to write this book. I was feeling empty, hopeless, and in total disbelief. I asked God in my prayers to somehow let me know he was real.

When I began writing this book, I got inspired and I started writing things that in a way I felt were not coming from me. It was more like I was reading instead of writing the book because I had all those questions, but I didn't have the answers. Part of the answers to the questions were coming in my dreams and parts were coming like someone was whispering through my mind, but I knew it wasn't me giving myself the answers. The answers were given very clearly, making complete sense in response to the doubts I had. I started telling my close friends about what was happening to me because it was an experience that I had never gone through before in my life.

One morning, I woke up ready to continue writing the book. I felt a little confused about writing this book and I said in my mind, Oh God, I don't know if what I am doing is right. I just don't want to mislead anybody or confuse anybody. How can I know that you are okay with what I am doing? On that morning there was a thought that came into my mind, like an answer, to not wear my reading glasses. I then said to myself, okay that must mean I should not be writing this book because I cannot read without my reading glasses. I will not be able to see anything. But the thought insisted that I not wear them. I listened to my thought and did not wear my glasses. To my surprise, I was able to read the book even better than I did while I had been wearing my glasses. With that I understood that it was okay for me to write the book. But then I had another question. What if there is something in the book that you don't want me to write. How will I know? Then, there came another thought saying to me that whenever there was something that I wasn't supposed to write it was going to be blurred and I would not be able to read it.

About a month after that, I commented to one of my neighbors that I was writing a book. I asked her to come to my house so I could show it to her. She came and I was showing her what I had written when we noticed one of the pages was blurred. I was scrolling up and down just to check if any other page was blurry, but that was the third page and everything else, up and down, was clear except for that page. My neighbor was next to me, looking at that page at the same time as I was, noticing it was blurry. I thought to myself that I was the only one who was seeing that page.

To my surprise, she was also seeing it, but I didn't know until she said to me, "Why is that page like that?"

That's when I realized she was also experiencing what I was seeing. I was happy to know that I had a witness of this. I had to explain to her why that page was like that. Later, when we told our other neighbor what happened, I saw disbelief in her face. She was thinking logically, she thought maybe it was taking long to upload the page. I asked her why it was then, that the pages below it were clear.

I continued to explain to her that there was something I needed to correct in that page and I found the mistake and fixed it. The mistake was the word "poseia" instead of the word "pensaba" in Spanish. I meant to say "When I was thinking about God," which is "Cuando yo pensaba en Dios." Instead I said "Cuando yo poseia a Dios," which was "When I used to possess God." God knows that was an honest mistake, not done on purpose, but he showed me I needed to correct it by blurring the page.

During this time I needed someone to help me with the proofreading and the neighbor who was, in a way, thinking logically and not believing what had happened with that page was helping me with the proofreading. I prayed to God to please allow her to see a sign that everything I was writing in this book was with his will and that miracles can happen. That morning there was a blurred line on one of the pages and I asked, God, allow her to see this line because she has been asking me for something to show her. I said, how can I know if God wants her to see it? I then thought, I'm going to call her. If when I come back this line is there the way it is, that means our Creator is allowing her to see this. If the line is clear, that means this was only for me to know. And I thought to myself, if that is the case that is okay because it's me who needs to believe before anyone else about this book.

I went to call her and she came with me right away. I showed her that page on the computer and she saw that line.

She exclaimed, "This cannot happen! How can this happen? This is not normal. This program, the one you're using doesn't have that feature the way the line looks."

She got closer to the computer just to check if her eyes were playing a trick on her. She was astounded, shaking her head in disbelief. But then she believed after she realized that it was true. She asked me a question, "Okay, I understand God wants you to fix this line. But then what is it that needs to be fixed or corrected?"

She tried to type onto the document to move

SONIA AHMED

the blurred line down or hoping to clear the lines. God then knew she believed that is when the line cleared and the sentence we needed to correct was that all the prophets came to prove that God existed with their own capacity. That was when I understood that no one is capable of doing anything without the spirit of God.

We all know that God exists and we all know that he has all kind of powers, that he can move mountains and perform miracles that would be too illogical to understand. But we all know that he can do it all, that there is no such thing as impossible for Him and when the time comes for him to reveal to you that he's real, you don't need to see him, but he can come in a form that you can understand. And yet we have a hard time believing that something like that can really happen. But to be honest with you I truly believe that that is our trial. That is the challenge that we have: to believe or not. This is a true story.

I went to pick up my kids from school that Friday at 3 P.M. After having driven my car the whole day long, I tried to start my car once again, but the ignition did not start. I tried to call AAA for service, but the signal in my phone was being interrupted. I was frustrated, but luckily I live about a block away from the school and I decided to walk back to my house, leaving the car in the school parking lot. I thought to

195

myself, I'll go drop off my kids and be back for the car. When I came back, it was a little dark, around 7 P.M. I tried to start the car again, but the battery was completely dead. It was not starting at all, just like when I had tried at 3 P.M.

I was frustrated; I raised my hands questioning God why this was happening. With my hands still in the air, away from the keys, which were in the ignition, I watched as the keys turned by themselves, turning the car on, on their own. Right after that, the lights from the car turned on, then the radio, too. I was amazed at everything because I was aware I did not turn the car on. I was frozen, trying to make logic of what was happening. How did that happen? I had been trying to turn the car on all this time and then it just suddenly turned on by itself.

There was a message in the car on the radio. I really did not pay attention to it because I didn't know at first if that was a regular radio station or if that was God trying to talk to me. I just had a thought in my mind, is this you who did it or what? The answer was *do you think I don't know about technology or cars?* With my mouth wide open, I tried to guess what was going on. The only thing that I can remember of that is that when I asked him when he was coming he said not to worry about it because Judgment Day is one-on-one.

I did not pay attention for the rest of the message because I was frozen. I felt so cold that I started shaking and my bones started to hurt. The message on the radio lasted about five minutes. First, the radio turned off, and then the ignition also turned off after the radio.

After that, I knew that it was him and that he was listening to me. I thought to myself, okay can I take the car now? Then in my mind, a thought said, try it. I tried to start the ignition, but I could not. It was completely dead. I tried about eight or ten times and not one of those times was I able to start the ignition again. I finally gave up and I said, okay I guess you're not going to allow me to take the car. So, I decided to go back to my house, leaving my car in the parking lot overnight. When I got to my house, I did not want to explain this to my kids because they were too young to understand what had happened. I thought that at first, but I then decided to tell them. I came in the living room and told my son and his friend about what had happened in the car. Suddenly, the TV turned on in the living room. They got scared so I thought, God don't send me messages in front of them. They are still young. Then, the TV turned off by itself. I went to bed, but I was in shock thinking about what was happening. I prayed that night asking to please let me know if it was really God who was doing all these things to me because I was not scared of anyone, any spirit or anything like that, but I was not interested in having any communication with anyone but him, our Creator. I wanted to make sure that all those things that were happening to me were coming from him – no one but him. On that night, he made me repeat all night that he was the Creator because he created everything on earth. And he was the Provider because he provides us with everything we need and that no one but Him can say that because everyone that was made by him knows how powerful he is. And no one but Him can say they are Him.

That night I understood that it was God who was giving me all the answers. The most beautiful thing I learned that day was that I am not special. Anyone, with no exceptions, can experience what I did if they have the same questions that I did. He can reveal to anybody, just like he did to me, in some way. They don't need to be Prophets, they don't need to think they are special or need to be special in order for this to happen to them, to know that he really exists. Even though it was a hard thing to believe that everything that was happening to me was true, it is true.

During that week, I was having a lot of visions during my sleep and also when I was awake. I learned that he can change lives in a moment as easy as when we delete pictures from our phones. That is how he does it in our life: knowing what is the next event to be without our permission or our knowledge.

END

When I began to write this book, I asked God to help me think because I didn't want to offend him. I didn't want to guide someone wrongly either. Because of this, I ask you to doubt what I have said and to start your own search, wherever you are. It is not good to believe what you see or hear. After all, the intention of this book is not to be right, because that is not the purpose because it wasn't my EGO that wanted to find the truth of GOD it was my soul for the freedom of my soul and my children and all the generations to come.

When I started to write, I deleted many things that were on my mind and without judgments requested our creator to allow me to know the truth not for my EGO, because I did not care to be right but to know the truth not only for me but for the rest of the world ; It is only so you can learn to know your soul because once you finally know it, you will realize the only thing you need to do is believe in our provider, God, let yourself go, and believe firmly. You need to ask in faith and in faith it will come to be. It doesn't matter if in the eyes of a doctor it is not realistically possible because doctors generally let themselves be guided by statistics, by previous patients. There is not one Doctor who will give you a diagnostic and say it with 100% security. They will tell you to go to another Doctor for a second opinion, even a third.

Many times, as bad as the news a Doctor gives us may be, we choose to believe in him, a human like us, not God. My question is, why do we believe a Doctor and not God? We come back to the same thing. It is because we see the doctor and the analysis, but we don't see God. We also don't see anything that can prove the doctor is wrong.

In one of the books I have read the description of faith is: Practically, the ability to believe in something firmly even if you can't see, touch, or feel it. You have the firmness that it is there even if you don't have the evidence that it is so. When you come to know the guide to the trail you need to go, it is easy to follow the path. In other words, when you are searching for God he will reveal himself, don't ask me how because I did not know what would happen to me before it happened. I just know it will happen because it works in his natural way, just like gravity. We don't understand gravity, but we know there is gravity. We cannot see it, but we know it's there. And it works every single time. I know I cannot see God, but I know he's there and I know he never fails and is there for everyone at every moment in everybody's life. I just know in my heart that I have nothing to lose by believing this and a lot to win.

Other words of being in faith are: to deny what you are seeing. An example is incredibility or denial; anything that is at that moment observed as reality within your mind or spirit. It is something that is coming and cannot be seen or confirmed by the world. This book is not about unifying religions, it is about unifying you with God because in one of my dreams that I had, God said to me that religion is a place where we just go and hang out with our friends or the people with which we have things in common. But the connection with God most likely happens anywhere at any given time because we are the temple and by going to the temple we think it is the church or place that we go to to pray. By thinking we cannot talk to God unless we go there is kind of like searching for God outside of ourselves. It is possible for us to go and find God there when we look within. That is why in that dream he said to me that it doesn't matter what religion we have or if we don't have a religion, it matters that we believe he exists and he's there for us. What our Creator wants is for us to be unified, one on one, with him because that is how our life can be changed: when we know who we are and where we are coming from. Sometimes we want to change the world and don't realize who we can and need to change is ourselves, individually because at the end of it all like in the beginning, we are one.

ACKNOWLEDGMENTS

Today is Thanksgiving

How beautiful to end this book on a day like today, to write the last part of the book <u>Unify</u>; to whom I dedicate this book.

I need to thank God, our Creator of all, first of all, for allowing me to write this book. It was a surprise to me that this book was in me, waiting to be born or discovered; it was there all this year, but I did not know it myself. I need to thank God for teaching me to see more than I was able to see before. I need to thank God for teaching me to hear more than I was able to hear before. I need to thank God for allowing me to feel more than I could feel before. I need to thank God for teaching me to discover what was just covered by him, for me to discover this beautiful surprise that was in me. I need to thank God for all the people that he has put in my path for one reason or another because all of them form part of my life, the life he gave me as a gift. I need to thank God for allowing all these brothers and sisters of my human family coming from you, our Creator, that helped me make this dream come true from the time I was born until the end of my passing life on earth, sharing this beautiful experience that we call life with this borrowed body to be visible to others.

I need to thank my mother for her last wish. She asked God as her last wish to give me wisdom to be able to help my family, those around me, and myself.

I need to thank my father for encouraging me to always do my best and for continually telling me, in a way, my destiny was to be successful and that I had no choice about that. And the only one that could stop me was God. He used to say to me, "Do not let others stop you, be yourself." And those voices became an echo in my life after my father was no longer alive.

I need to thank God for allowing me to forgive many people.

I need to thank God for giving me the family

that I have: my brothers and sisters Ana, Aura Marina, Eddy, Carlos, and my angel sister Maira.

I need to thank God for my husband Towzik Ahmed and the children that he allowed me to have: Omar and Ameer. I need to thank God for my husband's sisters and their families: Romana Wahid and Mona Faris for being a part of my life making sure I was fine on many occasions.

I need to thank Jose Aguirre for helping me with the Spanish part of the book Unify.

I need to thank my brother, Dr. Eddy Amilcar Novoa, for helping me with the Spanish book Unify and challenging me to make this book better.

I need to thank Daniela Jimenez for helping me with the translation of the book Unify.

I need to thank Lucy Andradc for helping me by proof reading the book Unify.

I need to thank future to be, with the blessing of God: Business administrator Ambreen Ahmed, for helping me by proof reading the book Unify

I need to thank Linda Naseteddin for proof

reading the book <u>Unify</u>.

I need to thank my friend Karen Al Hussaine for being part of my witness while I was writing the book and her support and challenging questions with the intention of finding nothing but the truth in the book <u>Unify</u>.

I need to thank my friend Rocio Medel for being there for me during the times of need in my life.

I need to thank Teresa and Mike Andrade for answering a lot of my questions about the Bible and helping me with an open mind just with the purpose of finding the truth of who we really are.

I need to thank Mr. and Mrs. Abdul and Rowena for answering some of my questions about the Quran with an open mind with the purpose of unifying people towards God.

I need to thank Mr. and Mrs. Ernesto and Gabriela Santiana for answering questions that I had in regards to The Tanakh (Torah) and for the time we spent together after that casual dinner sharing knowledge about Judaism.

I need to thank God for having as my witness

of one of the miracles Aishah Wahab when the TV turned on by itself and when it turned off after I mentally asked God to please turn off the TV because they were not ready to see the messages I was receiving. I was concerned because I thought they were too young to receive the messages with me. They may be scared; therefore the TV was turned off by the Unseen, Our Creator, immediately after I said that in my mind.

I need to thank my neighbors for being my neighbors.

I need to thank Nancy and Naser Long for their time and sharing with me their beliefs in regards to what this life is for them. At first I got the impression they had no beliefs in regards to God, Our Creator, because it is what they thought to themselves, but after talking with them for some time it was a nice surprise to me that deep inside there was a doubt in their hearts. And, yes, they had believed in God before, but there was a moment they lost hope and that took away their belief. I pray for them, for God to manifest to them just like it happens to me because they are both wonderful people.

I need to thank Antonio Banderas for helping me with my website and being creative and helping me with the cover of the book <u>Unify</u>.

I need to thank God for giving the thought in regards to the song "We Are One", created by Farhan Zand and a songwriter for Modern Talking. The lyrics are by Mina Jalali, for the music video, directed by Warner Bros and sung by Thomas Anders and Omid, music and video by Sony. I was praying for a song that could give the message that I need for the website of <u>Unify</u> and God listened to my prayers one more time, because not only did he give me the song that I needed, but the perfect video for the website, also. I thank all of them for being a part of the book <u>Unify</u>. In life there are no coincidences, therefore I thank all of them for being who they are, and being a part of the planet, Mother Earth.

I want to dedicate this book to God over all because he is the one and to humanity because we are one coming from one going back to one our Creator.

ABOUT THE AUTHOR

SONIA B. AHMED is a secretary, with specialization in marketing and advertising. She is currently working in Real State Business. She is the renowned author of the Spiritual, Self-development book Unify.

She is originally from Guatemala, currently an American citizen. After her father's death she decided to immigrate to the USA. When she made that decision she left with nothing in her hands, but with many dreams to fulfill in her heart.

Her book, Unify, allowed her to accomplish one of her many dreams: to overcome the struggle of understanding her purpose in life. That, along with the need of finding herself, is what led her write away the book of the story she wanted to become.

She is married to the man that she believes was destined to be her husband, Towzik Ahmed. She also has two children, Omar and Ameer. They have what they needed to have in order to be her family in this beautiful life full of challenges and beautiful moments. It was all made part of her life; just the way it needed to be to help her for her expansion which now is Unify.

Sequences of Life

For more information about Unify or Sequences of Life:

UnifyBooks@gmail.com
www.UnifyTheBook.com
P.O. Box 1299
Anaheim, CA 92815

www.ingramcontent.com/pod-product-compliance
Lightning Source LLC
LaVergne TN
LVHW051256080426
835509LV00020B/2995